American Heritage Series

Native American History Activities

Author: Schyrlet Cameron

Editor: Mary Dieterich

Contributor: Karl Mechem

Proofreaders: Alexis Fey and Margaret Brown

COPYRIGHT © 2022 Mark Twain Media, Inc.

ISBN 978-1-62223-880-4

Printing No. CD-405079

Mark Twain Media, Inc., Publishers
Distributed by Carson Dellosa Education

Visit us at www.marktwainpublishing.com

Table of Contents

Introduction to the Teacher

Native American History Activities is one of several books in Mark Twain Media's American Heritage Series for grades 5 through 8. This series is designed to provide students in grades 5 through 8 with opportunities to explore the significant events and people that helped shape our nation.

The study of history is important because if we don't know where we have been, we have no way to understand the present or predict the future. We should not try to hide from the past, even the unpleasant parts, so the bad decisions that were made have been included along with those that brought achievement and growth. Progress for our nation depends on how we as individuals and groups evaluate our decisions and react to the decisions of others. Wise decisions pull us up; foolish decisions push us down. As humans, we are all capable of both.

How the Book is Organized

The book text is presented in an easy-to-read format that does not overwhelm the struggling reader. Vocabulary words are boldfaced. The lesson provides challenging activities that promote reading, critical thinking, and writing skills.

The 28 lessons contained in *Native American History Activities* cover five units of study: *Indigenous People of North American, The New World, Trouble on the Frontier, Westward Migration,* and *American Indian Achievements*. The units can be used in the order presented or in an order that best fits the classroom or home school curriculum. Teachers can easily differentiate units to address individual learning levels and needs. Each lesson consists of two pages.

- **Reading Selection:** identifies the important events and people in Native American history.
- **Activity Page:** checks the reader's comprehension.

National and State Standards

Native American History Activities promotes the current national and state standards. It is written for classroom teachers, parents, and students. It is designed as stand-alone material for classrooms and homeschooling. Also, the book can be used as a supplemental resource to enhance the history curriculum for the classroom, independent study, or home tutorial.

Front Cover Identification:

(Center image) Grass Dancers at the 2007 National Pow Wow
(Clockwise from top right) Ballerina Maria Tallchief; Senator Ben Nighthorse Campbell; depiction of the Battle of the Little Bighorn by Charles Marion Russell; Black Elk and Elk of the Oglala Lakota; an Inuit family; Chief Joseph (Hin-mah-too-yah-lat-kekt) of the Nez Percé

Prehistoric Migration to the Americas

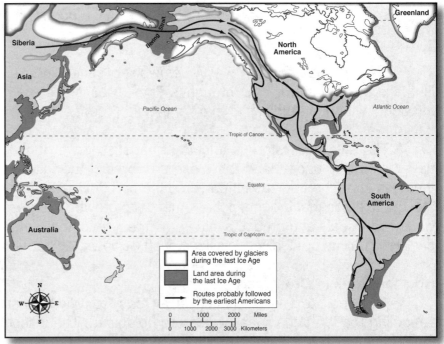

Although the names of those who first moved to North America are not recorded, we do know a little about them and how they traveled. The first people to arrive in the Americas did not sail here in large ships—they walked thousands of miles across Siberia in Asia to present-day Alaska in North America.

Scientists believe the Bering land bridge from Asia to North America was a route of animal and human migration about 30,000 years ago.

Last Ice Age

The earth has passed through several **ice ages**, a time of freezing temperatures. During the last Ice age, two-mile-thick sheets of ice called **glaciers** formed. These giant ice sheets covered the Arctic and Antarctic regions of the earth. The levels of the oceans lowered because much of the earth's water was trapped in the polar ice caps. The lower water level exposed a piece of land between Asia and North America. This land bridge was a thousand miles wide. Today this area is once again underwater and is called the Bering Strait. The **Bering Land Bridge** disappeared under the water when the ice caps thawed around 8,000 B.C.

Crossing the Bering Land Bridge

Scientists believe the land bridge was free of ice and covered in grass. Herds of hairy elephants called **mammoths** and giant bison from Asia came to graze. Stone Age people followed the grass-eating animals across the land bridge. This mass movement of people and animals from one region to another is called **migration**.

These early people depended on animals for food, clothing, and shelter. They knew how to use fire. Without it, they might not have survived. With it, they could stay warm and cook meat. These early people were the ancestors of the American Indians.

Migration

Small groups began arriving in North America about 30,000 years ago. As they traveled, groups might settle for a time in a place that offered good hunting or fishing. Some stayed for a year or two, or even many years, before moving on. Eventually, some of the group or their descendants continued the journey, following the migrating herds of animals they hunted into the eastern parts of North America. In time, some of these hunting people went as far south as the tip of South America.

Not all groups made the journey at the same time. Many waves of migrants crossed the land bridge during a period covering more than 25,000 years. When Christopher Columbus set sail from Spain in 1492, thousands of groups of people with many different cultures and languages lived in the Americas.

Name: Date:

Activity: Cause and Effect

Directions: Study the map and then answer the questions.

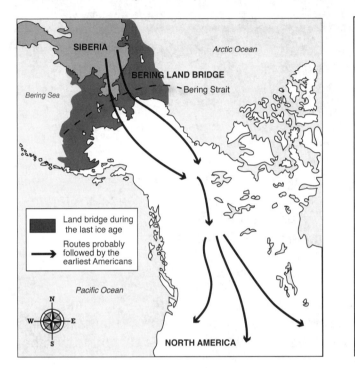

1. What was the name of the land bridge that connected Asia with North America?

2. In which direction did nomads migrate across the Bering Strait?

Directions: Complete the graphic organizer using information from the reading selection.

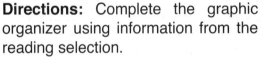

Causes:

Effects:

Early Cultures and Civilizations

Many scientists believe that early people **migrated**, or traveled, from Asia to North America during the last ice age. They crossed the **Bering Land Bridge** and began to spread out and settle in North America. These people then moved into Central and South America.

Ancestral Pueblo housing was built under the overhangs of cliffs.

The first people to live in a land are called **indigenous peoples**, or original settlers. Today, we refer to the first people who settled in the Western Hemisphere as **Indigenous Americans** or **Paleo-Americans**. *Paleo* is a prefix from the Greek language meaning "old." The indigenous peoples of North America are referred to as **Native Americans**. The first people to settle within the **contiguous**, or mainland, United States, are referred to as **American Indians**. The mainland of the United States consists of the 48 adjoining states.

Discovery of Agriculture

The Indigenous Americans were **nomads**, people having no permanent home. They traveled from place to place to find food. All the original settlers' food came from plants, animals and fish near where they lived. When the food supplies ran out, the people moved to another area to find a fresh supply.

When the Indigenous Americans learned **agriculture**, or how to plant and harvest crops and raise livestock, their way of life changed. This discovery allowed them to remain in one area for longer periods of time. Since they no longer had to move to find food, they built permanent villages. The people in these communities shared a way of life. They spoke the same language, followed similar customs, used similar tools, and had similar beliefs. The way of life shared by a group of people is called a **culture**. Agriculture also made the development of civilizations in both North and South America possible. A **civilization** has large cities, a complex government, and highly developed arts and science.

Early Cultures and Civilizations

- The **Aztec Empire** was based in what is now central and northern Mexico. They developed an advanced agricultural system.
- The **Mayan Empire** spread throughout present-day southern Mexico and Central America. The land included rugged highlands as well as dense swamps.
- The **Inca Empire** spread through parts of what are now Peru, Ecuador, Chile, Bolivia, and Argentina. The Incan land included deserts, fertile valleys, rain forests, and the Andes Mountains.
- The **Mound Builders** were a group of early people who built large dirt mounds. They lived from the present-day Great Lakes to the Gulf of Mexico and the Mississippi River to the Appalachian Mountains.
- The **Ancestral Pueblo** people lived in the desert area of the American southwest, where present-day Colorado, New Mexico, Arizona, and Utah join at one point.
- The **Hohokam** culture flourished in the hot dry desert of what is now Arizona.

Name: _____   Date: _____

Activity: Locating Information

Directions: Use the information from the reading selection to complete the page.

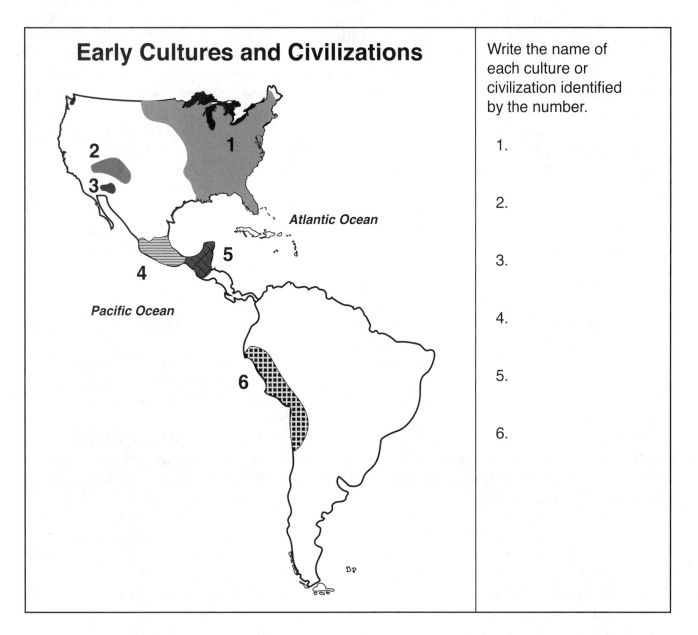

Early Cultures and Civilizations

Write the name of each culture or civilization identified by the number.

1.

2.

3.

4.

5.

6.

Fill in the Blanks

1. The way of life shared by a group of people is called a _____.

2. A _____ usually has large cities, a complex government, and

    highly developed arts and science.

Native American Cultural Regions

An **indigenous person** is one who originally inhabited a certain location. Anthropologists have divided the areas where the Indigenous People of North America lived into **cultural regions**. The regions are based on shared characteristics such as language, customs, and beliefs. Bands of people within the cultural regions are called **tribes**.

The **Northern Hunters** lived in northern arctic and subarctic regions of North America. The people in this region hunted caribou, polar bears, walrus, and whales. They included the Aleut and Inuit. The Aleuts lived in earth houses called **barabaras**. In the winter, the Inuit built ice block homes called **igloos**. In summer, many Inuit lived in animal-skin tents.

The **Northeast Woodland** tribes lived in the eastern part of the continent. In addition to hunting, fishing, and gathering, the people of the Northeast Woodlands grew corn, beans, and squash. They built wood houses called **longhouses**. The major woodland tribes included the Algonquian and Iroquois.

Southeast Woodland tribes lived in the southeastern region of the continent. These tribes were skilled farmers. They grew corn, squash, and beans. They also grew tobacco. Deer, bear, fish, squirrel, and rabbit were all hunted. Different tribes had different types of homes. In some cases, they would build a **wigwam**, a kind of shelter made of sticks and logs covered with grass. The tribes included the Cherokee and Seminole.

The **Plains** tribes lived in the west-central region of the continent. They lived in **tipis**, tent-like structures made of poles covered with animal hides. They relied on hunting herds of bison for food. Plains tribes included the Comanche and Sioux.

The **Pueblo** tribes lived in the southwestern United States and northern Mexico. They hunted small game such as rabbits and large game such as antelope. The main crop the Pueblo raised was corn. The people lived in houses made of **adobe**, a sun-dried clay brick. Pueblo tribes included the Apache and Navajo.

The **Pacific Northwest** tribes lived along the northwestern coast of North America. They lived in longhouses that could be up to 100 feet long and 25 feet wide. The longhouses had a log frame and were covered with thick cedar planks and bark. They were hunters and fishers. They also gathered seeds, berries, and nuts for food. The tribes included the Chinook and Tlingit.

The **California** tribes were known as "seed gatherers of the desert." Their diet included berries, nuts, seeds, and roots. The most typical houses were cone- or dome-shaped structures. They consisted of a pole frame covered with grass, brush, or bark. In some places, dwellings were covered with earth. The tribes included the Chumash and Yahi.

The **Great Basin** and **Plateau** tribes lived in the west-central region of what is now the United States and Canada. They hunted bison, deer, elk, and mountain sheep and caught salmon. The people also collected seed and root foods. They lived in tipis or grass-covered domed **wickiups**. The tribes included the Nez Percé and Shoshone.

The people of the **Mesoamerican** culture lived in present-day Mexico and Central America. The people grew a type of corn known as maize. Most homes were built of adobe bricks. The culture included the ancient Aztecs.

The **Central American** people raised maize along with vegetables such as beans and squash. They lived in huts made of stone or mud and covered with grass. The culture included the ancient Mayas in the Yucatan Peninsula. The ancient Mayas built huge pyramids, which are now ruins.

Name: _____   Date: _____

Activity: Locating Information

Directions: Use the information from the reading selection to complete the page.

Native American Cultural Regions

Multiple Choice

1. The Inuit built houses called
   A. barabaras.
   B. wigwams.
   C. igloos.
   D. tipis.

2. The Great Basin and Plateau tribes include the
   A. Apache and Navajo.
   B. Cherokee and Choctaw.
   C. Algonquian and Iroquois.
   D. Nez Percé and Shoshone.

Fill in the Blanks

1. An _____ person is one who originally inhabited a certain location.

2. A _____ region is based on shared characteristics such as language, customs, and beliefs.

3. Bands of people within the Native American culture regions are called _____.

4. The ancient Mayas built huge _____

True or False

Write the word TRUE if the statement is correct. If the statement is false, write the word FALSE and underline the word or statement that makes the sentence incorrect. Write the correct answer on the space provided.

_____ 1. The Plains tribes hunted bison.

_____ 2. The Pacific Northwest tribes were known as the "seed gatherers of the desert."

_____ 3. The Woodland tribes lived in houses made of adobe.

The Age of Exploration

The **Age of Exploration** began in the 15th century and lasted through the 17th century. It was a period of time when European nations began exploring the world by sea in search of new trading routes. The main purpose of European exploration was to make money. When the Ottoman Empire captured Constantinople in 1453, many existing trade routes to the **Far East**, India and China, were shut down. These trade routes were very valuable as they brought products such as spices and silk to Europe. Several nations sent expeditions to discover oceangoing routes to the Far East. An **expedition** is a journey or voyage by a group of people for the purpose of adventure and exploration.

Superpowers Spain and Portugal

The Age of Exploration began in the nation of Portugal under the leadership of a 15th-century Portuguese prince known as **Henry the Navigator**. If Portugal could find a sea route around Africa, they could trade directly with India and China. Around 1420, Henry sent out ships to map and explore the west coast of Africa. In 1488, **Bartolomeu Dias** of Portugal led the first European expedition around the southern tip of Africa. This opened the way for sea trade between Europe and the Far East.

Soon the Spanish wanted to find a trade route to India and China. Explorer **Christopher Columbus** thought he could sail west, across the Atlantic Ocean, to the Far East. Spanish monarchs Isabella and Ferdinand agreed to pay for Columbus' trip. At this time, the maps that Columbus used did not include the Americas.

In 1492, Christopher Columbus landed on an island in the Caribbean Sea and claimed the land for Spain. Columbus believed he had reached the East Indies and described the people he met as "Indians." The Indigenous People Columbus encountered were actually the **Taino**. Within a century of their first meeting with Columbus and Spanish settlement on the islands of the Caribbean, the Taino people were wiped out.

The two superpowers during the 15th century were Spain and Portugal. Both countries claimed the land discovered by Columbus. In 1494, the **Treaty of Tordesillas** solved the problem of who owned the land discovered by Columbus. Spain received most of the Americas, while Portugal received the land now known as Brazil in South America. The treaty also gave Spain and Portugal the right to claim any land of any people they conquered in the Americas. The results proved disastrous for the Aztec and Inca civilizations.

Spanish Explorers and Native American Civilizations

Spain sent explorers known as **conquistadors** to the Americas. They received financing from the king to explore and establish settlements in return for one-fifth of any gold or treasures discovered.

- In 1519, **Hernán Cortés** landed on the east coast of present-day Mexico while searching for gold. He soon learned of the great **Aztec Empire**. In 1521, the Spanish attacked and destroyed the Aztec capital of Tenochtitlán. The empire fell apart, and the Spanish seized control of the region.
- In 1524–25, **Francisco Pizarro** sailed the Pacific coast of South America. He searched for gold and found the **Inca Empire** in 1532 in what is known today as Peru. The Spanish took gold and silver from the Inca and killed their emperor, Atahualpa. Pizarro gained control of most of the Inca Empire and claimed the land for Spain.

Name: Date:

Activity: Cause and Effect

Directions: Use the information from the reading selection to complete the page.

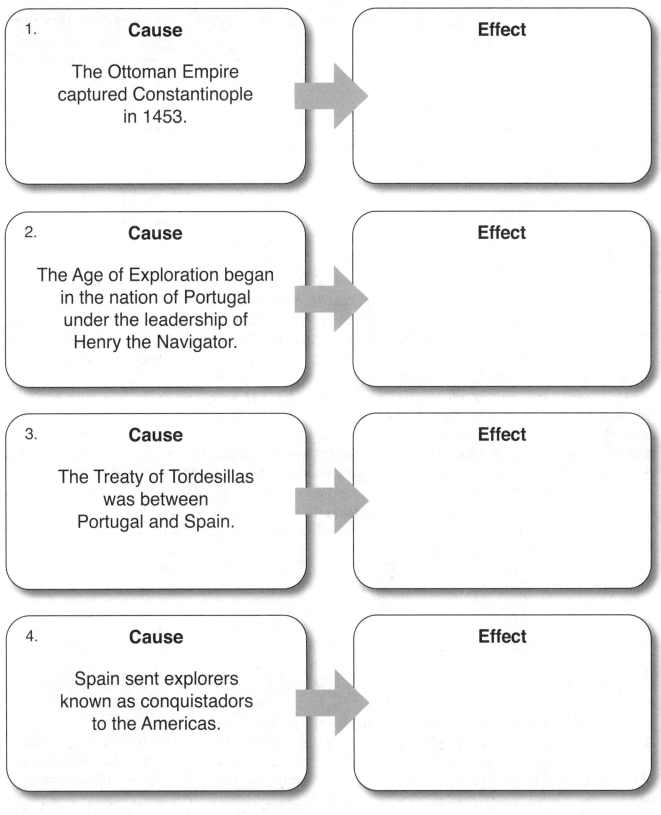

1. **Cause**

    The Ottoman Empire captured Constantinople in 1453.

    Effect

2. **Cause**

    The Age of Exploration began in the nation of Portugal under the leadership of Henry the Navigator.

    Effect

3. **Cause**

    The Treaty of Tordesillas was between Portugal and Spain.

    Effect

4. **Cause**

    Spain sent explorers known as conquistadors to the Americas.

    Effect

First Contact

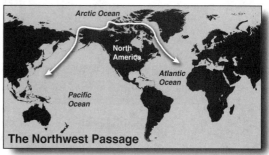

The Northwest Passage

It is likely that Viking explorers encountered Indigenous People of North America during their 10th-century settlement of Newfoundland. European explorers from England, France, and the Netherlands first made contact with the Indigenous People of North America in the 16th and 17th centuries. Explorers were searching for the **Northwest Passage**, a water route to Asia through North America.

English, French, and Dutch Explorers

Jacques Cartier was a French explorer looking for the Northwest Passage. Cartier claimed the land now known as Canada for France. On Cartier's first trip in 1534, he sailed along the coast of what is now Quebec, where he made contact with the Iroquois. His men kidnapped the two sons of Chief Donnacona, and Cartier took them with him to France. In 1535, Cartier brought the two young Iroquois back. He explored up the St. Lawrence River to near present-day Montreal. He then captured Donnacona and took him to France, where Donnacona died. In 1541, Cartier brought French settlers to establish a colony. When the Iroquois realized the French intended to settle, they became unfriendly.

In 1578, **Sir Francis Drake** became the first Englishman to navigate the Straits of Magellan, a sea route at the southern tip of South America linking the Atlantic and Pacific Oceans. Drake then sailed north along the west coast of the Americas, searching for a possible northwest passage. He landed near present-day San Francisco Bay, claiming the land for England. There he met and made friends with the Coastal Miwok. He continued the voyage and became the first Englishman to circumnavigate the globe in 1580.

English explorer **Sir Walter Raleigh** failed in his 1578 voyage to North America to find the Northwest Passage. In 1585, he sent ships to explore the Atlantic coast of North America and establish the first English settlement in the New World. The ship landed on Roanoke Island, part of the territory of the Carolina Algonquian-speaking people, known as the Roanoke. The Roanoke Island colony suffered from a food shortage and attacks by the Roanoke so the colonists returned to England in 1586. A second group arrived in 1587, but these colonists had all disappeared by the time a supply ship arrived from England in 1590.

Starting in 1607, English explorer **Henry Hudson** conducted four different expeditions searching for the Northwest Passage. On his third voyage while working for the Dutch, Hudson explored a river he named the Hudson River. Hudson traded with the Mohicans, and he was able to bring back corn, tobacco, and valuable furs to the Netherlands. His successful fur trading with the Mohicans led to more Europeans wanting to come and trade as well.

Samuel de Champlain was a French explorer who made many voyages to North America in the early 1600s in search of the Northwest Passage. In 1608, he established the first permanent French colony in North America, the city of Quebec on the St. Lawrence River. Champlain found the Algonquins and Hurons in a war with the Iroquois. Chaplain became an **ally**, or supporter, of the Algonquins and Hurons to protect the French fur-trading interests.

René Robert Cavalier de La Salle was also a French explorer searching for a water route to Asia. In 1682, Le Salle was the first European to navigate the Mississippi River to the Gulf of Mexico. He created a network of forts from Canada, across the Great Lakes, and along the Ohio, Illinois, and Mississippi Rivers. He formed numerous friendships with Native American tribes, many of which assisted and supported French settlers and military up to the French and Indian War of 1754.

Name: \underline{\hspace{5cm}}   Date: \underline{\hspace{5cm}}

Activity: Key Details

Directions: Use the information from the reading selection to complete the graphic organizer.

Jacques Cartier Key Details:	**Sir Francis Drake** Key Details:
Sir Walter Raleigh Key Details:	**Samuel de Champlain** Key Details:
Henry Hudson Key Details:	**René Robert Cavalier de La Salle** Key Details:

First Contact

Spanish Missions

Spain established the largest of the colonial empires in the New World. It claimed several islands in the West Indies, all of Mexico, most of Central America and South America, and present-day Florida, California, and the southwestern United States.

The Alamo was a Spanish Mission.

Spanish Missions

Missions were religious settlements set up in North America from the 1500s to 1800s by the Spanish. The main goal of missions was to convert Native Americans to Christianity and make them loyal Spanish citizens. Another motivation for the missions was to ensure that other European countries did not try to build settlements on land claimed by Spain.

Life at the Missions

The typical mission was a large area enclosed by stone walls. Inside the walls was a church. **Padres**, or religious leaders, managed the mission. Spanish soldiers stationed at the settlement protected people and mission properties.

The Native Americans lived in the missions until their religious training was complete. Then, the people were moved to homes outside the missions and expected to work in the fields or as cooks, gardeners, and laborers. Both men and women were expected to learn Spanish and attend the mission church. Those who ran away were often tracked down and returned.

Native American Resistance

Frequent rebellions against the Spanish and the missions erupted throughout what would become Texas, New Mexico, southern Arizona, and California. Revolts ended with many deaths of missionaries, settlers, and Native Americans.

The first missions established in New Mexico and present-day Chihuahua, Mexico, were the first to face Native American rebellion. From 1599–1620, tribes of the Sierra Madres rebelled against Spanish rule and mission life.

In 1680, the Pueblo Rebellion erupted in New Mexico. It was an uprising against Spanish missions and rule. The revolt by the Pueblo tribes, along with the Apache, ended Spanish rule in New Mexico for 12 years.

Mission San Diego de Alcalá, located in present-day San Diego, was the first Spanish Mission in California. It was established in 1769 by Junípero Serra, a Franciscan monk. The Tipai-Ipai tribe was resistant to mission life. In 1775, members of the tribe attacked the mission. It was burned down but was rebuilt as a fort.

End of the Mission System

By 1821, Mexico had won its independence from Spain. In 1833, the Mexican government passed a law that ended the mission system. This included the missions in California since California was part of Mexico in the early 1800s. During the 1846–48 war with Mexico, the United States military used the missions as bases.

Name: _____   Date: _____

Activity: Summarizing

Directions: Use the information from the reading selection to complete the graphic organizer.

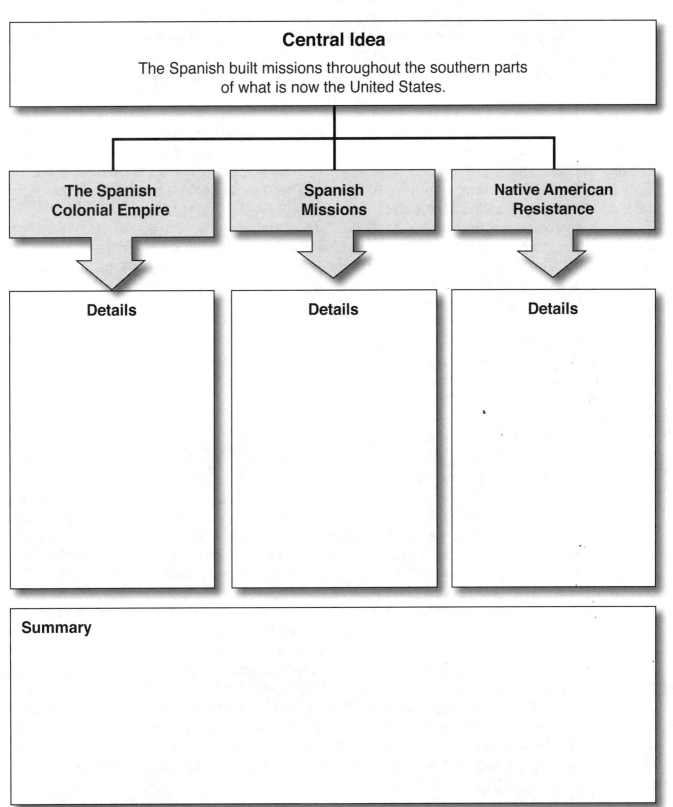

Central Idea

The Spanish built missions throughout the southern parts
of what is now the United States.

**The Spanish
Colonial Empire**

**Spanish
Missions**

**Native American
Resistance**

Details

Details

Details

Summary

The Powhatan Confederacy

The Algonquian people of the Northeast shared the same language and culture. The people lived by hunting, trapping, and fishing. They gathered roots, nuts, wild rice, fruit, and berries. Many groups also grew corn, beans, squash, and tobacco.

The **Powhatan Confederacy** was a union of 30 Algonquian tribes that occupied the coast of Virginia, Chesapeake Bay, and Southern Maryland. The Confederacy was formed by the powerful chief of the Powhatan tribe, **Wahunsenacah**, also known as **Powhatan**.

Powhatan Confederacy and Jamestown

Jamestown was the first permanent English settlement in North America. In 1607, the Virginia Company of London sent three ships with 104 men and boys to North America to establish a coastal settlement for the company. The three ships sailed into the Chesapeake Bay. They built James Fort, along with several houses. The new settlement was named after King James I and later was called Jamestown.

It is estimated that from 14,000 to 21,000 Native Americans lived in eastern Virginia when the English colonized Jamestown. The tribes of the Powhatan Confederacy were the first to make contact with the settlers. When the English arrived, Powhatan wanted to trade food in exchange for weapons and tools. But as the settlers took over more land, the relationship between the settlers and the tribes was strained.

The Anglo-Powhatan Wars

The **Anglo-Powhatan Wars** were a series of wars between the English settlers of Virginia Colony and the Algonquin tribes of the Powhatan Confederacy.

The **First Powhatan War** was from 1610 to 1614. Most of the English settlers joined the expedition to get rich. They did not know how to fish, hunt, or farm. The colony relied on the Native Americans for food. Chief Powhatan helped the British settlers through their first winters. But the good relations did not last. In 1609, trade relations became strained because a severe seven-year drought stressed food supplies for everyone in the region. In 1609, Powhatan reduced trade, attempting to starve the colonists out of the area. When the English demanded food, Powhatan attacked James Fort. Hostilities continued as new settlements were established, taking more land. During this time, colonists learned to cultivate tobacco, which was exported to Europe. The demand for tobacco increased the demand for more land. In 1613, **Pocahontas**, daughter of Powhatan, was captured by the English during hostilities. She married tobacco planter John Rolfe, bringing peace and ending the war.

The **Second Powhatan War** was from 1622 to 1626. In 1618, Chief Powhatan died, and his younger brother **Opechancanough** took control of the Confederacy. The highly profitable tobacco trade led to the further takeover of Powhatan land, resulting in attacks on the colonists throughout the area. The English fought back. In 1632, peace was made, ending the war. The Powhatan people were banned from most of the Chesapeake area.

The **Third Powhatan War** was from 1644 to 1646. In 1644, Opechancanough launched another attack on the English settlers to drive them from the area. The third war ended when Opechancanough was captured and killed. The new leader signed a peace treaty that dissolved the Powhatan Confederacy and gave most of their **ancestral**, or tribal, land to the colonists.

Name: Date:

Activity: Textual Evidence

Directions: Use the information from the reading selection to answer the questions. Support your answers with specific details and examples.

1. **Who were the Algonquian people of the Northeast in North America?**

   Answer:

2. **What was the Powhatan Confederacy?**

   Answer:

3. **What caused the conflict between the Jamestown colonists and the Powhatan Confederacy?**

   Answer:

4. **What were the results of the Anglo-Powhatan Wars?**

   Answer:

The Wampanoag Confederacy

The **Wampanoag Confederacy** was a union of over 30 Algonquian-speaking Native American tribes who lived in the eastern part of present-day Massachusetts and Rhode Island. The Wampanoag consisted of about 15,000 people before the arrival of Europeans. They were hunters, gatherers, farmers, and fishers.

By 1620 when English settlers arrived, the Wampanoag Confederacy was led by **Massasoit** of the Pokanoket tribe. Chief Massasoit and the Wampanoag Confederation helped the English colony of Plymouth survive in the New World.

The Great Dying

Ships from England had been fishing and trading in North American waters since the 1500s. They brought foreign illnesses the Indigenous people lacked immunity to fight. Between 1616 and 1619, smallpox spread throughout the region, and only a fraction of the Wampanoag population survived. This time became known as the **Great Dying**.

Sculpture of
Chief Massasoit
by Cyrus Edwin Dallin

Samoset and Squanto

Samoset was a leader of one of the Wampanoag tribes. Samoset learned to speak English from European travelers who had been visiting the northeastern coast of America since 1497.

Tisquantum, commonly known as **Squanto**, was a member of the Patuxet tribe. In 1614, Squanto was kidnapped by English explorer Thomas Hunt and taken to Europe, where he learned to speak English. Squanto returned to America in 1619 to his village, only to find that his tribe had been wiped out during the "Dying Time." He went to live with the Wampanoag.

The Arrival of the *Mayflower*

In 1620, 100 settlers and 50 crew members on the *Mayflower* landed in Cape Cod Bay in present-day Massachusetts. The ship lay anchor at the spot the settlers named "Plymouth." The first winter in Plymouth, almost half the Pilgrims died.

In the spring of 1621, while Samoset was visiting the chief, Massasoit sent Samoset and Squanto to arrange a meeting with the Pilgrims. After exchanging greetings and gifts, Chief Massasoit and leaders of the Plymouth settlement signed the **Pilgrim-Wampanoag Peace Treaty**, a peace treaty that lasted for more than 50 years.

King Philip's War (1675–1678)

Chief Massasoit died in 1662, and his son **Metacom**, known as **King Philip** by the English, became the leader of the Wampanoag people. At the same time, the English settlements were expanding further and further into Wampanoag land. Chief Metacom led an uprising to drive out the colonists. During the 14-month conflict, thousands of Native Americas were killed, wounded, or captured, and the Wampanoag tribe was destroyed. Metacom fled to Mount Hope in present-day Bristol, Rhode Island, where he was killed by the English.

Name: _____   Date: _____

Activity: Cause and Effect

Directions: Use the information from the reading selection to complete the graphic organizer.

Cause   ## Effect

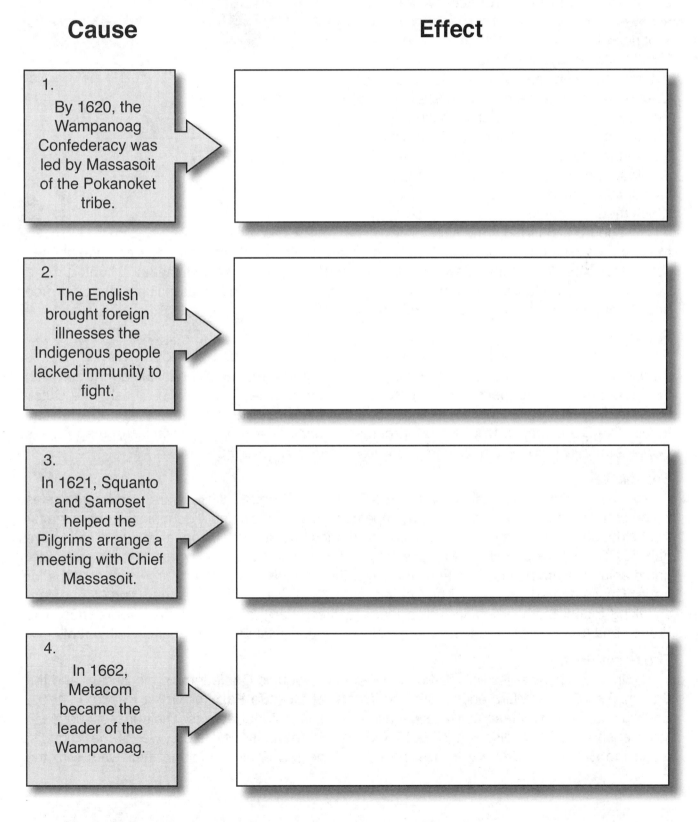

1.

By 1620, the Wampanoag Confederacy was led by Massasoit of the Pokanoket tribe.

2.

The English brought foreign illnesses the Indigenous people lacked immunity to fight.

3.

In 1621, Squanto and Samoset helped the Pilgrims arrange a meeting with Chief Massasoit.

4.

In 1662, Metacom became the leader of the Wampanoag.

The Iroquois Confederacy

The **Iroquois Confederacy** was a powerful **alliance**, or group, of Native American tribes in the 1600s and 1700s. The Confederacy was made up of five nations: the Cayuga, Mohawk, Oneida, Onondaga, and Seneca. The Tuscarora tribe joined later. These people spoke the Iroquois language and lived in villages in the northeastern woodlands area in what is present-day New York State. They called themselves the Haudenosaunee, which meant "People of the Longhouse."

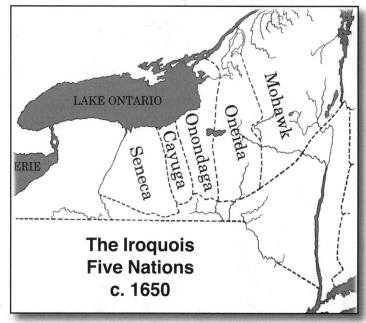

The Iroquois Five Nations c. 1650

The Iroquois lived in homes called **longhouses**. The houses were built of wood covered with sheets of elm bark. Each one housed several families. The people grew corn, beans, and squash. They also fished and hunted.

The Iroquois lands were surrounded by Algonquian-speaking tribes including the Shawnee and Huron, who were not part of the Iroquois Confederation.

Fur Trade

In the 1600s, the fur trade was a very important industry in North America. Native Americans would hunt game animals and trade the **pelts**, animal skins including the fur, with the Europeans. Beaver pelts were in great demand in Europe. The French, British, and Dutch competed against each other to get these pelts and formed alliances with the Native American tribes. The French made **treaties**, or agreements, with the Algonquin, enemies of the Iroquois Confederacy. The Iroquois mainly traded with the Dutch and later the British.

Beaver Wars

The **Beaver Wars**, also known as the French and Iroquois Wars, were a series of battles from about 1629 to 1698. The Iroquois competed with the Huron and Algonquin to control the fur trade. The beaver population in the Iroquois territories had almost disappeared due to excessive hunting. The Iroquois decided to move into Huron hunting territory, where beaver and other game animals were abundant. During the wars, the Iroquois Confederacy took control of the fur trade. They defeated the Huron. The Confederacy attacked French settlements and Algonquian-speaking tribes. Many tribes, including the Shawnee, were forced from their homelands. The French and their allies responded with attacks on Iroquois villages and English settlements.

The Great Peace

In 1698, peace was established between the Iroquois Confederacy, the British, and the French. The Beaver Wars ended with the **Treaty of Grande Paix**, or **Great Peace**, in 1701. English and French representatives signed it, as well as 39 tribal leaders. The treaty did not push the French out of Iroquois territory, but it did expand the influence and power of the Iroquois. Later, the British colonies would use the help of the powerful Iroquois in their wars with the French.

Name: Date:

Activity: Textual Evidence

Directions: Use the information from the reading selection to answer the questions. Support your answers with specific details and examples.

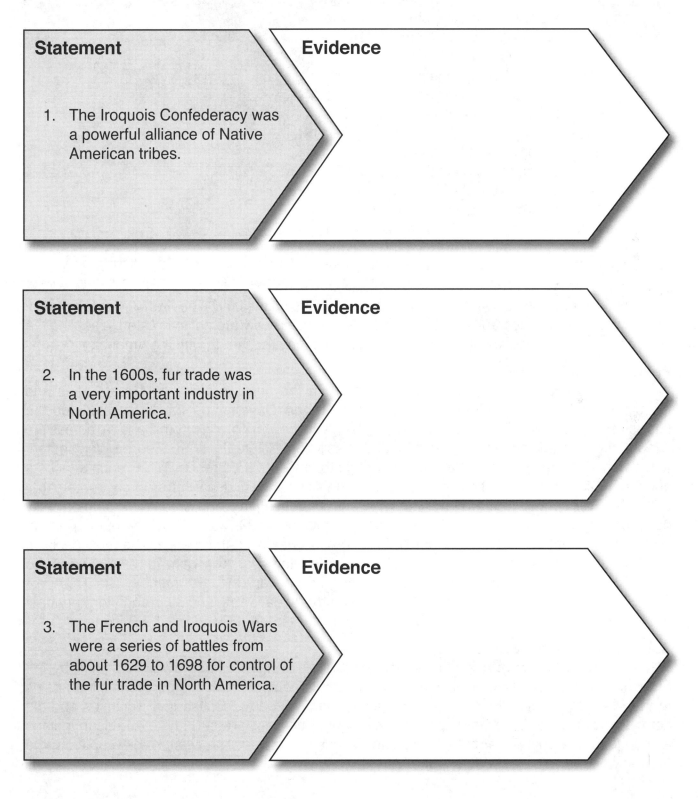

Statement

1. The Iroquois Confederacy was a powerful alliance of Native American tribes.

Evidence

Statement

2. In the 1600s, fur trade was a very important industry in North America.

Evidence

Statement

3. The French and Iroquois Wars were a series of battles from about 1629 to 1698 for control of the fur trade in North America.

Evidence

French and Indian War

The thirteen British colonies were located along the Atlantic coast. To the north of the British colonies was New France (Canada); French Louisiana lay west of the Mississippi River. To the south was Spain's colony, Florida. All three nations saw the importance of having American Indian **allies**, or supporters. The Algonquins backed the French. The Iroquois supported the English. Spain's allies were the Seminoles and Creek. When war came, the three European nations recruited their Native American allies as scouts and warriors.

Many American Indians lived on the land of the Ohio River Valley between the French and British colonies. All three groups claimed the Ohio River Valley territory. Each group had its own reasons for wanting to control the land. The American Indians had lived on the land for centuries and depended on its resources to survive. They wanted to trade with the Europeans but did not want them to build settlements on the land. The French wanted control of the waterways and to trade with the American Indians. They were not interested in settling the land. The British wanted to build settlements, farm the land, and trade with the American Indians.

French and Indian War

French explorers were the first Europeans in the areas around the Great Lakes and the Ohio and Mississippi Rivers. In 1682, **René Robert Cavalier de La Salle** navigated the Mississippi River to the Gulf of Mexico. He established a network of forts from Canada, across the Great Lakes, and along the Ohio, Illinois, and Mississippi Rivers. In 1754, George Washington, along with 150 Virginia militia, was sent by Britain to drive out the French. The French attacked, and the Virginians were forced to retreat. This skirmish was the first in a series of encounters that led to the **French and Indian War**. After two years of fighting in North America, Britain officially declared war on France on May 17, 1756. Soon Spain joined the war on the side of the French.

Britain sent some of its best generals to fight the war in North America. The most decisive battle of the war was fought outside Quebec on the **Plains of Abraham** in 1759. There, the British defeated the French, ending major fighting in the war in North America. The **Treaty of Paris** was not signed until February 10, 1763. The treaty gave England all French territory east of the Mississippi River except New Orleans. Spain surrendered Florida to the British.

Settlements to the West

After the treaty was signed, British troops took over the forts previously owned by the French. British colonists expected to expand their settlements west of the Appalachian Mountains to the Mississippi River. Many American Indians considered the British their enemies and did not want colonists to build settlements on their land. The British regarded the American Indians as conquered people rather than allies. Soon, tensions between the two groups erupted into a frontier war known as **Pontiac's War**.

Name: Date:

Activity: Cause and Effect

Directions: Use the information from the reading selection to complete the graphic organizer.

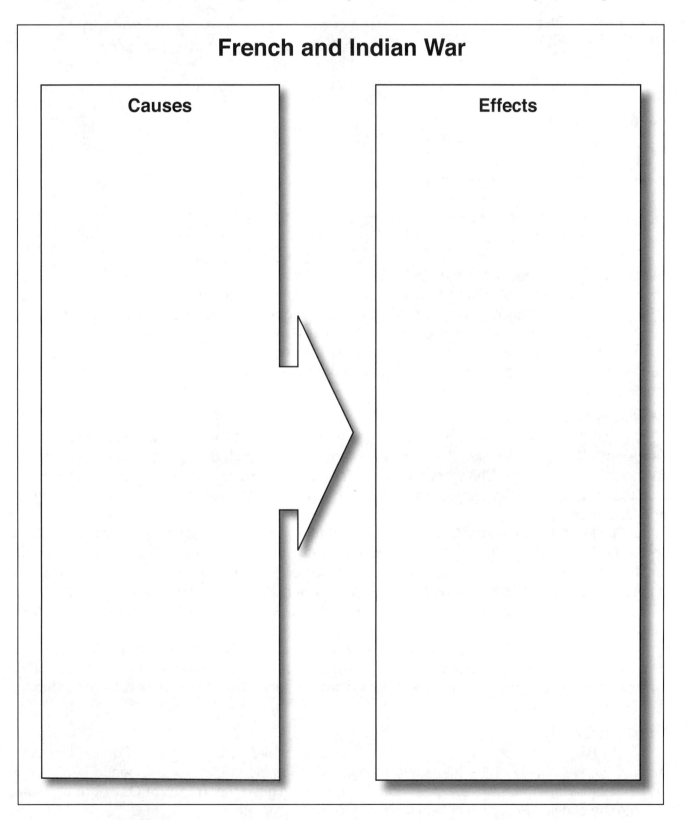

French and Indian War

Causes

Effects

Pontiac's War

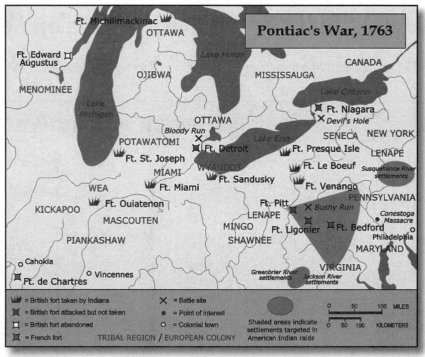

Pontiac's War, 1763

On February 10, 1763, the **Treaty of Paris** ended the French and Indian War. The treaty made Britain the ruler of Canada and the land between the Appalachian Mountains and the Mississippi River.

Settlements to the West

After the Treaty of Paris was signed, British troops took over the forts previously owned by the French. With French control broken, British colonists expanded their settlements to the "West." At that time, the **West** meant the area from the Appalachian Mountains to the Mississippi River in what was once territory claimed by France. Many American Indians lived on this land. They had lived on the land for centuries and depended on its resources to survive. They considered the British their enemies and did not want colonists to build settlements on their land. Before long, the American Indians living in the territory found themselves increasingly dissatisfied with the British control of the land and expansion of settlements.

Pontiac's War

Pontiac was born around 1720 in present-day Ohio. By 1747, Pontiac had became a war leader of the Ottawa people. The Ottawa supported the French during the French and Indian War. After the war, the Ottawa people were friendly with British settlers. As more and more settlers arrived, Chief Pontiac realized the British were trying to take control of land belonging to the Ottawa people.

In 1762, Pontiac organized a **confederation**, or group, of other Native American tribes in the Great Lakes region to stop the British. He planned surprise attacks on British forts and settlements. On May 7, 1763, Pontiac led an attack on Fort Detroit. This attack is considered the first battle of what is known as **Pontiac's War**. During the summer, the Shawnee, Wyandot, Seneca-Cayuga, and Lenape (Delaware) raided British settlements along the Pennsylvania and Virginia frontiers.

In October 1763, King George III issued a royal proclamation about the frontier. The **Proclamation of 1763** forbid any settlements west of the Appalachian Mountains. However, the settlers ignored the law and continued building settlements. The American Indians continued to fight settlers over the land.

Treaty of Oswego

In the autumn of 1764, the British military launched attacks against Pontiac's forces, ending the war. Many of the tribes surrendered. Pontiac did not agree to a peace treaty until 1766. Pontiac met with the British at Fort Ontario and signed the **Treaty of Oswego**, officially ending the conflict. Pontiac received a pardon for his role in the war.

Name: _____   Date: _____

Activity: Locating Information

Directions: Use the information from the reading selection to complete the graphic organizer.

Settlements to the "West"	Explain

Pontiac's War	Explain

Proclamation of 1763	Explain

Treaty of Oswego	Explain

The American Revolution

The **American Revolutionary War** was fought from 1775 to 1783. It was a time when the British colonists in America rebelled against the rule of Great Britain and King George III. When the war began, more than 250,000 Native Americans lived east of the Mississippi River. As fighting between the British and colonists increased, both sides called on the Native Americans for support.

Choosing Sides

King George III and the British Parliament decided to raise money to pay for the cost of the French and Indian War by taxing the American colonists. They reasoned it had cost money for the British government to defend the colonies during the war, so it was only right that they pay their fair share. The taxes made many colonists angry because they had no representation in Parliament to vote against the taxes or speak for the interest of the colonies. In 1775, the colonists began their fight for independence.

American Indians worried about how to protect their homeland while continuing to trade with both the British and the colonists. The more than 80 American Indian Nations east of the Mississippi River chose different strategies. Some remained **neutral**, did not take sides. Most of the nations sided with the British. A few allied with the colonists. Many who took part in the war conducted raids on supply lines, attacked settlements, and fought alongside soldiers in numerous battles throughout the war.

In the Ohio Valley, the Lenape (Delaware) tried to stay out of the conflict. In 1778, the local **militia**, or armed force, killed White Eyes, leader of the Lenape. In 1782, the militia attacked the unarmed Moravian people. Afterward, the Lenape tribes allied themselves with the British.

In 1759, a series of conflicts between the Cherokee and the colonial militia known as the Cherokee Wars had begun in Virginia and spread to North Carolina and further southward. Peace treaties forced the Cherokee to give up millions of acres of land to settlers. Unhappy with the outcome, they joined the British in the Revolutionary War, hoping to keep what land they had left.

The Shawnee people were divided. Some wanted to remain neutral. Others wanted to join forces with the British, who they believed would prevent the colonists from building more settlements on tribal land. Chief Cornstalk led those who wished to remain neutral, while war leaders such as Chief Blackfish and Blue Jacket joined the Cherokee against the colonists.

Of the six nations that belonged to the Iroquois Confederacy, four, including the Mohawk, sided with the British, while the Oneida and Tuscarora supported the American colonists. Leaders Cornplanter, Red Jacket, and Joseph Brant led the Iroquois, who were loyal to the British and participated in raids.

End of War

The American Revolution ended with a victory for the American colonists. The **Treaty of Paris** that declared peace was signed on September 3, 1783, in Paris, France. Britain recognized the independence of the United States. The new nation received all the territory between the Atlantic Ocean and the Mississippi River and between the Great Lakes and Florida. The American Indians were considered a conquered people throughout the entire country and were eventually forced to give up most of their land. Even the Iroquois nations who had fought with the Americans were convinced to sell their lands and move west as more and more settlers intruded on their territory.

Name: _____   Date: _____

Activity: Locating Information

Directions: Use the information from the reading selection to answer the questions.

1. What was the American Revolutionary War?

    Answer:

2. What were the main causes of the American Revolution?

    Answer:

3. What role did the American Indians play in the American Revolutionary War?

    Answer:

4. What was the result of the American Revolutionary War?

    Answer:

The Northwestern Confederacy

On July 13, 1787, the United States Congress created the **Northwest Territory**. Also known as the Ordinance of 1787, the ordinance established a government for the territory and outlined the procedure for admitting a new state to the Union. The region included what is now present-day Illinois, Indiana, Michigan, and Wisconsin, as well as part of Minnesota. At the time, the territory was a vast wilderness populated by American Indian cultures, including Lenape (Delaware), Miami, and Shawnee.

The Northwestern Confederacy Tribes in the Northwest Territory.

Little Turtle

Michikinikwa was a leader of the Miami people of the Great Lakes region during the 1700s. He was born about 1752 in present-day Indiana. Michikinikwa was allied with the British during the American Revolution, and in 1780 he led the defense of his village against attacking French troops. The English called Michikinikwa **Little Turtle**.

Little Turtle's War (1785–1795)

The **Northwestern Confederacy** was a union of American Indian tribes in the Great Lakes region of the United States created after the American Revolutionary War. The confederation consisted of the Miami, Shawnee, Lenape (Delaware), Mingo, Wyandot, Cherokee, Ottawa, Ojibwa, and Potawatomi.

Little Turtle's War, also known as **The Northwest Indian War**, was a conflict between the United States and the Northwestern Confederacy for control of the Northwest Territory. Little Turtle played a leading role in the efforts of the confederacy to stop the westward expansion of settlers rapidly crossing the Appalachian Mountains to the Northwest Territory. The confederation led by Little Turtle began raiding settlements.

In response to these raids, President George Washington ordered military action. In 1790, General Arthur St. Clair led troops into Miami and Shawnee lands. Little Turtle and his followers defeated General Josiah Harmar's forces in the battle that became known as **Harmar's Defeat**. In 1791, General Arthur St. Clair led 2,000 United States soldiers in an attack on Confederacy tribes in western Ohio. Little Turtle led his followers to victory in the battle now known as **St. Clair's Defeat**.

On June 30, 1794, Little Turtle led the confederation in an unsuccessful attack against General Anthony Wayne at Fort Recovery. Following this defeat, Little Turtle encouraged the nations of the confederation to negotiate with the United States for peace. Shawnee war chief Blue Jacket and others refused and continued fighting. On August 20, 1794, Blue Jacket and his followers were defeated at the **Battle of Fallen Timbers**, ending the war.

In August 1795, Little Turtle signed the **Treaty of Greenville**. The Northwestern Indian Confederacy gave the United States much of Ohio and parts of Illinois, Indiana, and Michigan.

Name: _____

Date: _____

Activity: Locating Information

Directions: Use the information from the reading selection to complete the graphic organizer.

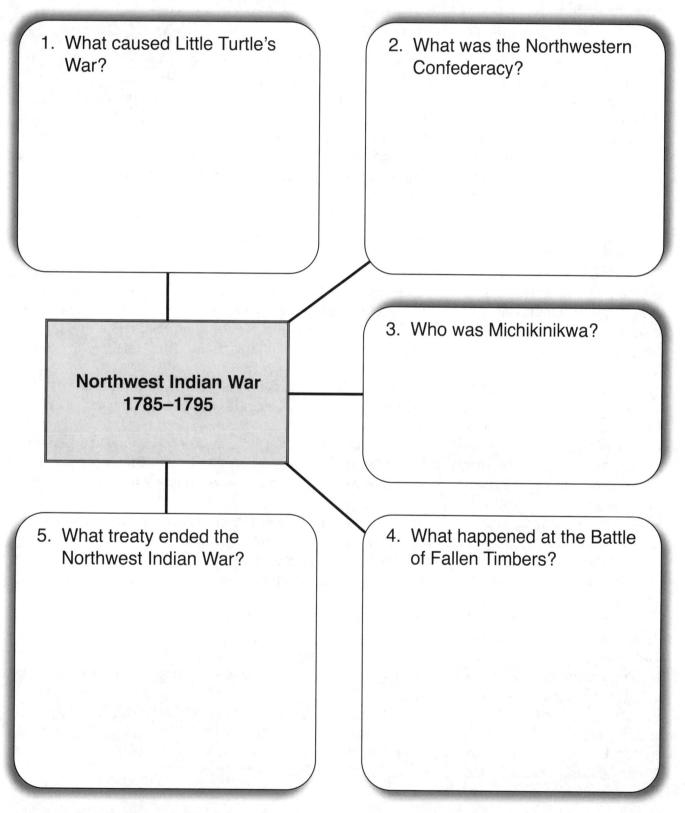

1. What caused Little Turtle's War?

2. What was the Northwestern Confederacy?

Northwest Indian War 1785–1795

3. Who was Michikinikwa?

5. What treaty ended the Northwest Indian War?

4. What happened at the Battle of Fallen Timbers?

Tecumseh

Tecumseh was a Shawnee leader. He dedicated his life to uniting American Indian tribes east of the Mississippi River and north of the Ohio River to fight westward expansion into the Northwest Territory.

Ohio Valley Confederacy

Tecumseh was born in 1768 in present-day Ohio. He grew up during a time of almost constant conflict between the Shawnee and American settlers. In 1774, his father was killed by American soldiers during **Lord Dunmore's War**. The conflict between the American Indians and settlers was fought over land ownership in the Ohio Valley.

Tecumseh became an important leader while still a young man. He participated in many raids on American settlements and took part in several battles, including the **Battle of Fallen Timbers** in 1794. A victory for the United States military, the battle ended the **Northwest Indian War**, also known as **Little Turtle's War**. In 1795, the **Treaty of Greenville** was signed. Tecumseh disputed the treaty over the surrender of tribal lands and refused to sign. After, Tecumseh tried to unite the tribes of the Ohio Valley against settlers.

Tecumseh met with considerable success in his efforts to unite the tribes. His younger brother, Tenskwatawa, called the "Shawnee Prophet," greatly aided Tecumseh in his efforts. The name "Prophet" was given to Tenskwatawa because he had once overheard British officers discussing an eclipse of the sun was due on a certain date. He returned to his tribe and told his people that, at a certain time, the sun would die and then later return. After this event, he was known as the Prophet.

Tecumseh, his brother, and some members of his tribe left the Ohio area around 1808. They went to the Indiana Territory close to where the Tippecanoe and Wabash Rivers joined and founded the village of Prophetstown.

In 1809, William Henry Harrison, governor of the Indiana Territory, convinced several tribal leaders to sign the **Treaty of Fort Wayne**. The treaty gave the United States three million acres of American Indian land. Tecumseh opposed the treaty, questioning whether the leaders had the authority to sell the land.

In 1810, Tecumseh began recruiting tribes to join his confederacy, which united the Shawnee, Potawatomi, Kickapoo, Winnebago, Menominee, Ottawa, and Wyandot Nations to fight the expansion of the United States. His goal was to form an independent nation of Americans Indians east of the Mississippi. A gifted speaker, Tecumseh traveled constantly in an effort to convince the tribes to unite.

In 1811, Governor William Henry Harrison, concerned with the alliances formed by Tecumseh, attacked Prophetstown at Tippecanoe while Tecumseh was away recruiting. At the **Battle of Tippecanoe**, Harrison destroyed the village. The Shawnee withdrew after the battle, leaving behind guns with English markings. To settlers, this was proof that the American Indian tribes were being armed by the British.

The **War of 1812** was a conflict between the United States and the United Kingdom over a disagreement in trade practices. During the war, Tecumseh and his followers joined the British. In 1813, at the **Battle of the Thames**, Tecumseh was killed. On December 24, 1814, Great Britain and the United States signed the **Treaty of Ghent**, ending the war.

Name:

Date:

Activity: Key Details

Directions: Complete the graphic organizer with key details from the reading selection.

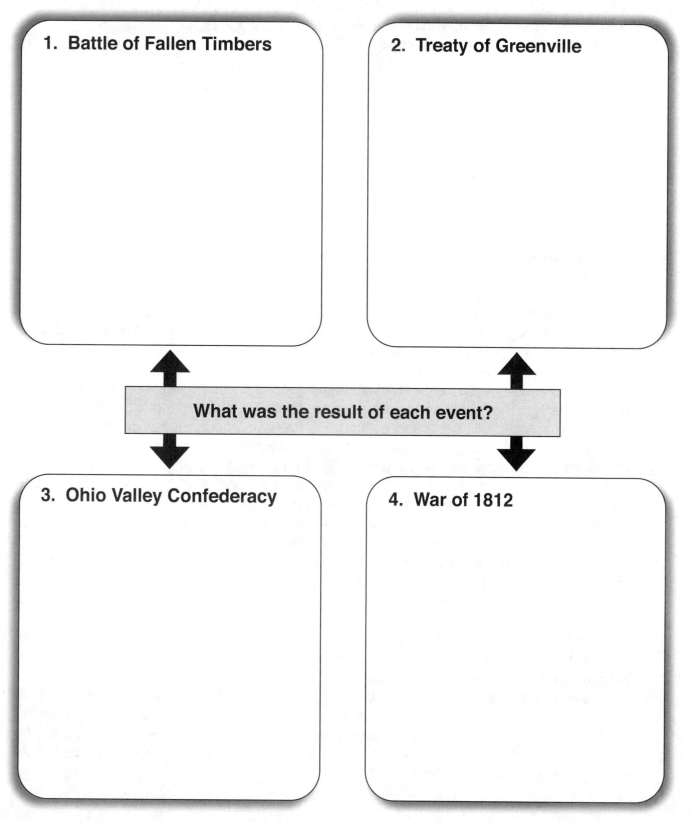

1. **Battle of Fallen Timbers**

2. **Treaty of Greenville**

What was the result of each event?

3. **Ohio Valley Confederacy**

4. **War of 1812**

American Indian Cultures of the West

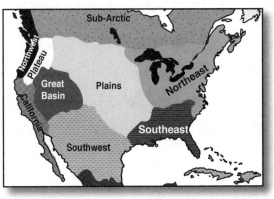

Many American Indian groups lived in what became United States territories west of the Mississippi River. They had very distinctive **cultures**, behaviors shared by a group, such as a language, customs, beliefs, and religion.

Cultures West of the Mississippi

1. The **Plains tribes** lived on the vast grasslands of the west-central region between the Mississippi River and the Rocky Mountains. The tribes included the Comanche, Sioux, and Blackfoot. Plains peoples were **nomads**, people with no permanent homes but who moved from place to place, finding food and resources along the way. The Plains people followed the buffalo herds for food. The hides were used to build **tipis**, portable tents made of animal skins on a frame of poles.

2. The **Southwest tribes** lived in what is now the southwestern region of the United States and northern Mexico. The Southwest tribes include the Pueblo, Apache, and Navajo. Most of the people combined farming with hunting and gathering. The Pueblos lived in houses known as **pueblos**. The dwellings were made of stone and **adobe**, sun-dried clay. The Navajo made **hogans**, round houses made of stone, logs, and earth. The Apache built **wickiups** made of brush and also used tipis.

3. The **Plateau tribes** lived in the northwestern region of what is now the United States. The land spread between the Rocky Mountains and the Cascade Mountain Range. Tribes included the Nez Percé, Flathead, and Yakama. Their diet included roots, berries, and wild game such as deer, elk, bear, and caribou. Fish was an important part of their diet also. They lived in tipis covered with animal skins or mats woven from grass.

4. The **Northwest tribes** lived along the coast of the Pacific Ocean from what is now the southern border of Alaska to northwestern California. Pacific Northwest tribes include the Chinook, Haida, and Tlingit. The men were hunters and fishers. The women gathered seeds, berries, and nuts for food. They built rectangular homes made of cedar. The homes were portable and could be taken down and moved to a new location.

5. The **Great Basin tribes** lived in the west-central region of what is now the United States and Canada, a desert region that stretches from the Rocky Mountains west to the Sierra Nevada Mountains. The Great Basin tribes include the Western Ute, Paiute, and Shoshone. The people were nomads. Their diets included roots, seeds, and nuts. Salmon was an important food source. It was dried or smoked for later use. They hunted bison, deer, elk, and mountain sheep. Some tribes used horses when hunting. The people built brush windbreaks in the summer and wickiups in the winter.

6. The **California tribes** lived in the area that includes most of what is now known as California and the northern part of the Mexican state of Baja California. Tribes included the Chumash, Promo, and Yuma. Their diets included berries, nuts, seeds, and roots. They hunted wild game such as rabbits and deer. House types varied throughout the California tribes. The most typical home was a wickiup.

Name: _____ Date: _____

Activity: Categorizing Information

Directions: Use information from the reading selection to complete the chart.

American Indian Cultures West of the Mississippi				
Culture	**Location**	**Tribes**	**Home**	**Diet**
Plains				
Southwest				
Plateau				
Northwest				
Great Basin				
California				

Manifest Destiny

The United States population grew from more than five million in 1800 to more than 23 million by mid-century. This population explosion increased the need to expand into new territory west of the Mississippi. **Manifest Destiny** was a widely held belief in the 19th-century. Many people believed the growth of the United States throughout the American continent was both a right and a duty.

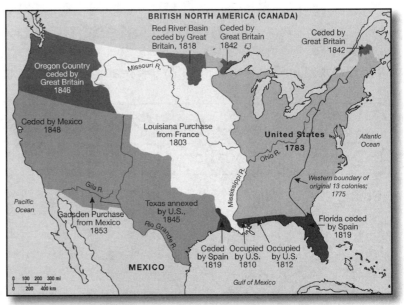

Manifest Destiny Causes Problems

One of the problems with expansion to the west was the fact that the land was home to countless American Indian cultures. Indigenous populations suffered through armed conflict with settlers and the United States Army over land. Eventually, many tribes were forced to relocate to reservations. A **reservation** is an area of land for American Indian tribes to live on and use. Reservations were created by treaties. **Treaties** were agreements between American Indian tribes and the United States government.

The United States Gains New Territory

The United States expanded its territory by treaty, war, and land purchase.

- **1803**: The United States doubled the size of the nation with the **Louisiana Purchase** from France for $15 million. Eight present-day states were created in their entirety from the Purchase: Louisiana, Missouri, Arkansas, Iowa, North Dakota, South Dakota, Nebraska, and Oklahoma. It provided most of the land for the present-day states of Colorado, Kansas, Montana, Minnesota, and Wyoming.
- **1845**: **Texas** had become an independent republic after war with Mexico in 1836. Texas was **annexed**, or taken over, by the United States and became the 28th state in 1845.
- **1846**: The **Oregon Treaty** was signed between the United States and Britain. The treaty established the 49th parallel as the border between the United States and British-owned Canada. In 1848, Congress formally established the land as the **Oregon Territory**. The territory includes the present-day states of Washington, Oregon, and Idaho and parts of Montana and Wyoming.
- **1848**: The nation expanded again after the **Mexican American War**. The land **ceded**, or surrendered, to the United States by Mexico was referred to as the **Mexican Cession**. The territory was organized as California, Utah Territory, and New Mexico Territory, which includes the present-day states of California, Nevada, Utah, most of Arizona, and parts of New Mexico, Colorado, and Wyoming.
- **1853**: The United States paid Mexico $10 million for the **Gadsden Purchase**, a strip of land along the southern edge of the present-day states of Arizona and New Mexico. The purchase established the Mexico-United States border.

Name: _____   Date: _____

Activity: Locating Information

Directions: Use the information from the reading selection to complete the graphic organizers.

Manifest Destiny	Definition
	Problems for American Indians

United States Expands Westward	1. Explain: Louisiana Purchase
	2. Explain: Texas Annexed
	3. Explain: Oregon Treaty
	4. Explain: Mexican American War
	5. Explain: Gadsden Purchase

Sacagawea and the Corps of Discovery

Sacagawea was a Shoshone woman who accompanied the **Corps of Discovery** from 1804 to 1806. Also known as the Lewis and Clark Expedition, explorers traveled from the northern plains through the Rocky Mountains to the Pacific Ocean and back. Sacagawea's skills as an interpreter were invaluable to the expedition team and the American Indians they encountered.

Sacagawea

Sacagawea was born around 1788. A member of the Shoshone tribe, she grew up in the region of what is now Idaho. In 1800, she was kidnapped by the Hidatsa tribe during a buffalo hunt. Around 1803, the Hidatsa traded Sacagawea to French-Canadian fur trader **Toussaint Charbonneau**. Later she became his wife.

The Lewis and Clark Expedition

In 1803, President Thomas Jefferson arranged a deal with Napoleon Bonaparte, the ruler of France, for the purchase of 820,000 square miles of land for $15 million. Known as the **Louisiana Purchase**, this deal nearly doubled the size of the United States.

Statue at the Sacagawea Interpretive Center in Salmon, Idaho

The Louisiana Territory was the home of thousands of American Indians.

President Jefferson chose **Meriwether Lewis** and **William Clark** to lead an expedition to explore the territory and find a water route from the Missouri River leading west to the Pacific Ocean. The expedition left St. Louis, Missouri, May 14, 1804. They sailed west and north on the Missouri River through Missouri, Iowa, Nebraska, South Dakota, and North Dakota. They had an unfriendly encounter with the Teton Sioux in South Dakota and then continued north to the Mandan villages near what is now Bismarck, North Dakota. The expedition spent the winter there. Toussaint Charbonneau, Sacagawea, and their baby traveled with the expedition when it left **Fort Mandan** in 1805. Sacagawea was extremely helpful to the explorers. She knew several American Indian languages. Later, she acted as the interpreter to bargain for horses from the Shoshone.

The Corps of Discovery traveled west on the Missouri River from Fort Mandan. The boat in which Sacagawea was sailing nearly capsized when a storm hit. She saved important papers, instruments, and medicines from being lost in the river. In appreciation, Lewis and Clark named a branch of the Missouri River for Sacagawea.

After the near-disaster, the expedition traveled north by land through the Rocky Mountains, where they met the Nez Percé people, who helped them with food and shelter. The group then floated down the Columbia River and reached the Pacific Ocean on November 15, 1805. The expedition spent the winter at **Fort Clatsop**. On March 23, 1806, the explorers left Fort Clatsop on their return journey. Sacagawea and Charbonneau left the group at the Mandan villages. Lewis and Clark reached St. Louis on September 23, 1806. The journey home had taken six months.

Sacagawea died at the age of 25 on December 22, 1812, at Fort Manuel, in present-day South Dakota after giving birth to a daughter. William Clark became the guardian for her son Jean-Baptiste and daughter Lisette. From 2000 to 2008, the United States Mint produced a dollar coin in her honor. The coin featured an image of Sacagawea carrying her infant son.

Name: Date:

Activity: Locating Information

Directions: Use the information from the reading selection and the map below to complete the graphic organizer.

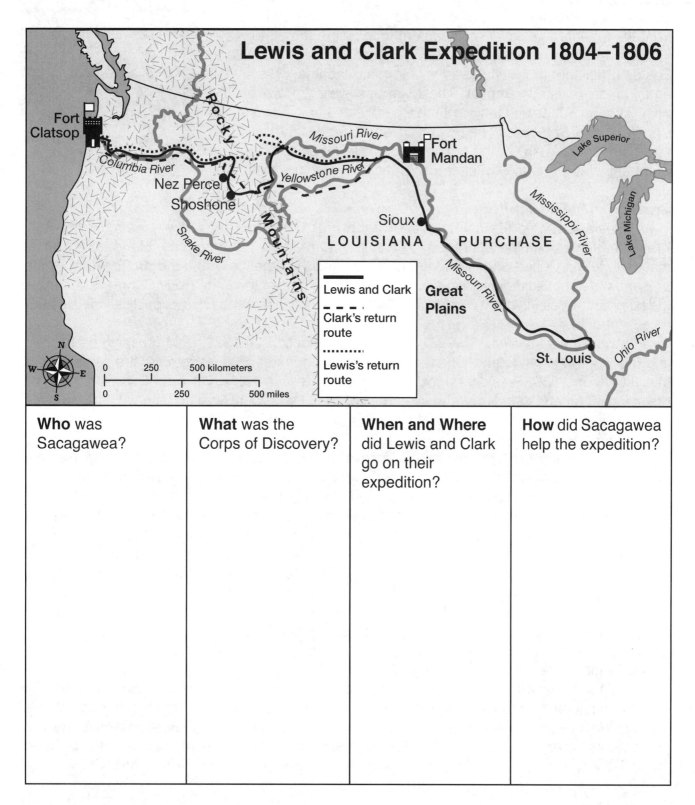

Who was Sacagawea?	**What** was the Corps of Discovery?	**When and Where** did Lewis and Clark go on their expedition?	**How** did Sacagawea help the expedition?

The Five Civilized Tribes

The American Indians in the United States came under increasing pressure in the 1820s to give up their tribal land and move west of the Mississippi River. The United States Government used **treaties**, or agreements, as one way to remove American Indians from their lands. The small northeastern tribes were forced to leave valuable lands and relocate to lands considered worthless by settlers. The southeastern tribes who lived in Georgia, Alabama, Mississippi, and Florida resisted removal. These groups were known as the Five Civilized Tribes and included the Cherokee, Creek, Chickasaw, Choctaw, and Seminole. They were called "civilized" by the white settlers because many of the members of these tribes had adopted European ways, and they often traded peacefully with the settlers.

Chief Osceola, leader of the Seminole people of Florida

Creation of Indian Territory

Settlers wanted the rich farmland of the Five Civilized Tribes to plant cotton. In 1824, President James Monroe approved the first plan to remove tribes from their land. In a special message to the United States Senate, he requested the creation of the **Indian Territory** in the present states of Oklahoma, Kansas, Nebraska, and part of Iowa. In 1825, Congress reserved the land for the resettlement of American Indians to the west of the Mississippi River in present-day Oklahoma.

Andrew Jackson won the 1828 presidential election. In 1829, gold prospectors flooded into the Cherokee lands in northern Georgia. The Cherokee tried to remove the settlers from their lands. In 1830, President Jackson signed the **Indian Removal Act**. This plan involved resettling all American Indians who lived east of the Mississippi River on land west of the river. This law forced the Cherokee and other tribes to leave their lands and relocate to land in the Indian Territory.

In the winter of 1831, the forced removal of the Choctaw to land in the Indian Territory began. The government had agreed to feed and clothe the people during their journey, but the money was never spent on the provisions. Many were barefoot; most had no coats or blankets. It made no difference; they were forced to travel on foot across the frozen Mississippi River.

The **Seminole War** of 1835 began when the United States Army arrived in Florida to enforce a treaty signed by some Seminoles to give up their land. The Seminoles refused to leave the land. Their leader, **Osceola**, was captured in October 1837 and died on January 30, 1838. After his death, most of his followers surrendered and relocated west to Indian Territory.

The Creeks were put in chains and forced from their homes in 1836 by United States soldiers. About 3,500 died of hunger and exposure before they reached their new territory. The following year, the Chickasaw were also forced to leave their tribal lands and relocate west to Indian Territory.

In 1838, General Winfield Scott and an army of 7,000 men forced the Cherokee people from their homes without warning and moved them into camps. They were only allowed to take the clothing they were wearing. An estimated 17,000 Cherokee began their relocation journey to present-day Oklahoma, known as the **Trail of Tears**. About one-fourth of those who started died along the way. It took nearly six months for those who lived to reach their destination.

Name: _____   Date: _____

Activity: Timeline

Directions: Use the information from the reading selection to complete the timeline.

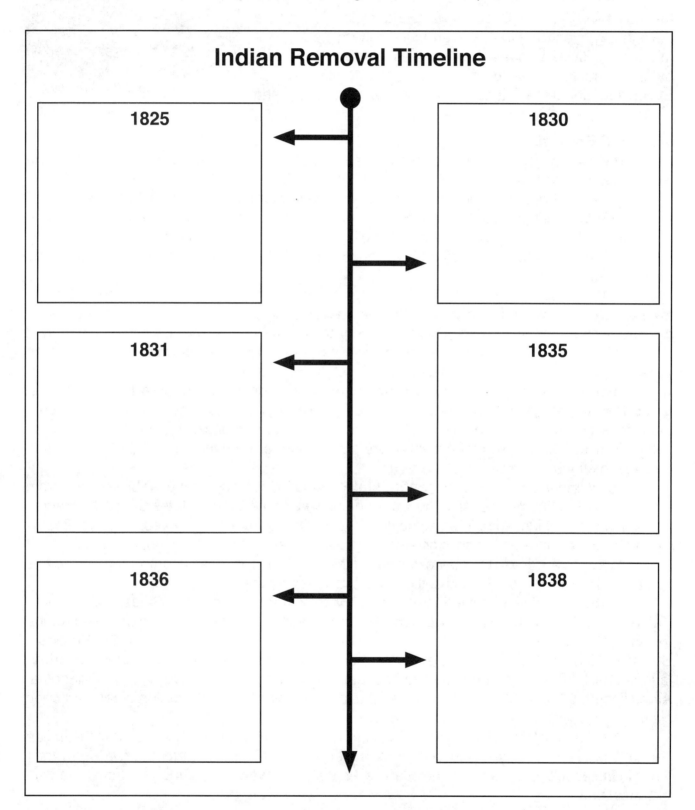

Indian Removal Timeline

1825	1830

1831	1835

1836	1838

American Indians Struggle

Westward expansion, the movement of settlers into the American West, began in the mid-1800s. Fueled by the belief in Manifest Destiny, westward expansion had a devastating effect on the American Indians living west of the Mississippi River. **Manifest Destiny** was a widely held belief by Americans in the 19th-century that the growth of the United States throughout the American continent was both a right and a duty.

Oklahoma Land Rush in 1893

Westward Expansion

The westward expansion of the United States started in 1803 with the **Louisiana Purchase**. The size of the United States instantly doubled when President Thomas Jefferson completed the Louisiana Purchase, buying a massive territory of around 828,000 acres of land west of the Mississippi River from the French for $15 million. To deal with the American Indian populations, the United States developed a policy of forcibly removing them from their lands. By the 1840s, the United States Army and the various tribes in the Plains region were in a continual state of war.

In 1848, gold was discovered at **Sutter's Mill** in California. As the news spread, people from all over the world swarmed to California, devastating the land. Native Americans found their traditional food sources depleted. Starving, they turned to raiding the mining towns and settlements. By 1853, California began placing its remaining American Indian population on **reservations**, tracts of land set aside for American Indians to live on.

In 1862, Congress passed the **Homestead Act**, opening the West to **homesteaders**, giving land to settlers who would farm it for a specified period. The lure of free land brought thousands of new settlers to the Great Plains, where many American Indians lived. As more settlers arrived, the people of the plains were pushed farther from their tribal lands or crowded onto reservations.

The completion of the **Transcontinental Railroad** in 1869 made it possible to travel from the east coast to the west coast of the nation in one week. The United States Congress granted millions of acres of land to railroad companies. According to **treaties**, or agreements, ratified by Congress, these lands belonged to different American Indian nations. The construction destroyed hunting grounds and led to the near extinction of the buffalo. In response, many American Indians damaged the tracks and attacked settlements supported by the railroad line.

In 1834, Congress created the **Indian Territory** in the present-day states of Oklahoma, Kansas, Nebraska, and part of Iowa. Congress promised the area would be a permanent refuge for American Indian tribes moved from their eastern homelands. However, in 1889, President Benjamin Harrison authorized the settlement of the **Unassigned Lands of Indian Territory**, land not assigned to one of the many tribes removed to the territory in present-day Oklahoma. An estimated 50,000 settlers raced across the land; all the allotted 1.9 million acres had been claimed by sunset.

In 1890, Congress established the **Oklahoma Territory** on unoccupied lands in the Indian Territory, breaking a 60-year-old pledge to preserve this area for the tribes forced from their lands in the east. **Land rushes** in the 1890s eventually removed most of the land from American Indian control.

Name: _____   Date: _____

Activity: Cause and Effect

Directions: Use the information from the reading selection to complete the graphic organizer.

Westward Migration

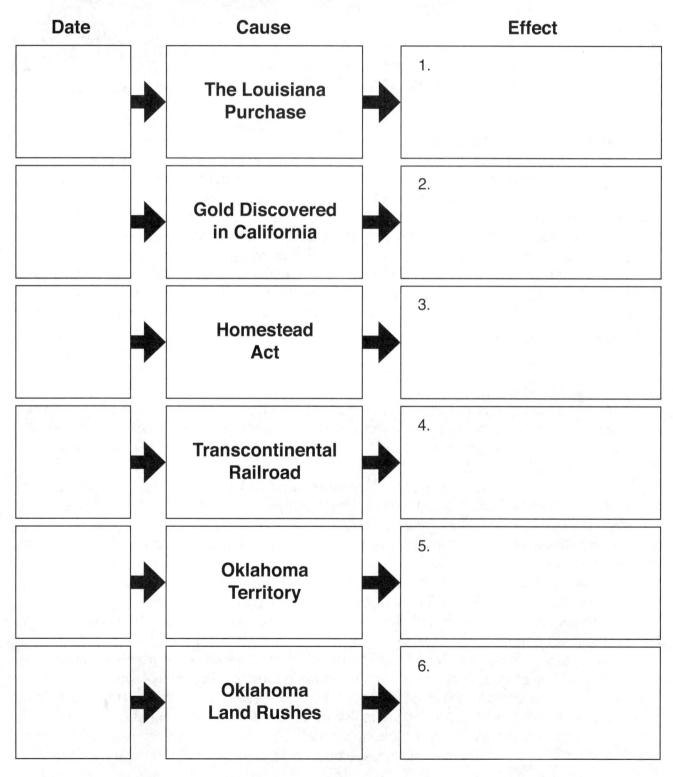

Date	Cause	Effect
	The Louisiana Purchase	1.
	Gold Discovered in California	2.
	Homestead Act	3.
	Transcontinental Railroad	4.
	Oklahoma Territory	5.
	Oklahoma Land Rushes	6.

The American Bison

It is believed that **American bison**, often referred to as buffalo, crossed over a land bridge that once connected the Asian and North American continents. Through the centuries, buffalo moved southward, eventually reaching as far south as Mexico and as far east as the Atlantic Coast, extending south to Florida. But the largest herds were found on the **Great Plains** and prairies from the Rocky Mountains east to the Mississippi River and from the Great Lakes in Canada to Texas.

Bison can weigh up to 2,000 pounds.

The Plains People and the Bison

The **Plains** was a vast grassland. The grass in the area fed great herds of buffalo. The largest group of American Indians lived in the Plains area. The people were nomadic, meaning they did not stay in one place but moved frequently, finding food and resources along the way. The people of the Plains followed the buffalo. The meat was their main source of food. The hunters killed only what they needed, using every part of the animal for food, clothing, shelter, and tools. The bison was also used in many spiritual ceremonies of the various Plains tribes.

When the Native Americans began using the horse, it changed their way of life. For centuries, the people of the Plains hunted buffalo on foot. The horse was brought to the New World by Spanish settlers. By the 1800s, the American Indians had learned to use horses, and they were gradually obtained by the Plains tribes. Horses made it much easier to travel and hunt buffalo.

Buffalo Herds Destroyed

The first Europeans to come to the Plains were trappers and fur traders. They traded manufactured goods, such as guns, knives, hatchets, beads, and wool blankets, for beaver, raccoon, fox, mink, deer, and even bear skins to make warm clothing. In the early 1800s, the trade moved on to buffalo robes.

In 1862, Abraham Lincoln signed the **Homestead Act of 1862**. This law opened huge amounts of land in the Plains to settlement. Unfortunately, many people at the time wanted to eradicate the buffalo to take away the livelihood and well-being of the American Indians. Some government officials thought destroying bison herds would help defeat American Indians who resisted the takeover of their lands.

Between 1863 and 1869, the **Transcontinental Railroad** was constructed across the Plains. This also decreased the buffalo populations. As crews worked their way across the Plains, hunters shot buffalo to provide food for the workers, often taking only the best meat and leaving the rest unused.

Later, train companies offered tourists the chance to shoot bison from the windows of their coaches. The animals they killed were left to rot in the sun. People even held bison-killing contests to see who could kill the most animals in the shortest amount of time. **Buffalo Bill Cody** reportedly shot more than 4,000 in two years. By 1883, both the northern and the southern herds had been destroyed. By the early 1900s, fewer than 300 wild buffalo remained in the United States and Canada out of the millions that had once lived on the North American continent.

Name: _____   Date: _____

Activity: Locating Information

Directions: Use the information from the reading selection to complete the page.

Multiple Choice
1. What effect did westward expansion have on the population of American bison?
   A. Westward expansion caused an increase in population.
   B. Westward expansion caused a decrease in population.
   C. Westward expansion had no effect on the population.
   D. Westward expansion stabilized the population.

2. Read the sentence from the text and answer the question.

   > *Unfortunately, many people at the time also wanted to eradicate buffalo to take away the livelihood and well-being of the American Indians.*

   Which word is a synonym for <u>eradicate</u> as it is used in the sentence?
   A. preserve
   B. protect
   C. shelter
   D. destroy

Question/Answer
3. Question: Who was a legendary hunter who was hired to slaughter thousands of buffalo?

   Answer:

4. Question: Where did the American Bison mainly live in the United States?

   Answer:

5. Based on the reading selection, what were **four** major events that contributed to the near extinction of the buffalo? Write your answer in the box below.

The Civil War

The **American Civil War** was fought from 1861 to 1865. It was a conflict over states' rights and slavery. When Abraham Lincoln was elected president in November 1860, there were 33 states in the **Union of the United States of America**. After he took office in 1861, eleven states in the southern part of the country decided to **secede**, or withdraw, from the Union. These states formed their own nation, the **Confederate States of America**. American Indian loyalties varied during the Civil War and were often motivated by a common desire to protect tribal lands and their way of life.

Ely Samuel Parker was a member of General Ulysses S. Grant's staff. Left to right: Parker, Adam Badeau, General Grant, Orville Elias Babcock, Horace Porter

Native Americans Take Sides

Although most tribes remained neutral in the conflict, approximately 28,000 American Indians participated in the Civil War as both Union and Confederate soldiers. A majority of American Indian nations fought for the Union, including the Shawnee, Iroquois, and Huron. More than 7,000 American Indians from the Indian Territory participated in the Confederate Army, as both officers and enlisted men. Most men came from the Cherokee, Chickasaw, Choctaw, Creek, and Seminole Nations.

One of the early battles in the Civil War that involved American Indians took place in 1862 at Pea Ridge, Arkansas. **Stand Watie** of the Cherokee held the rank of Colonel in the Confederate Army. He formed the **2nd Cherokee Mounted Rifles** and led the regiment at the battle. The **Battle of Pea Ridge** was a decisive victory for the Union Army. Watie went on to lead his troops in 18 battles. In 1864, he was promoted to the rank of Brigadier General. Stand Watie surrendered to Union troops in June 1865. He was the last Confederate general to surrender.

The most famous American Indian unit in the Union Army was **Company K of the 1st Michigan Sharpshooters**. A **company** was the basic unit in a Civil War army. Companies were named with the letters A–K. Company K was made up of 139 men and one officer from the Ottawa, Lenape (Delaware), Huron, Oneida, Potawatomi, and Ojibwa tribes. The company fought in several major battles, including the Battle of the Wilderness and Spotsylvania.

Ely Samuel Parker was a member of the Tonawanda Seneca tribe. He fought at Vicksburg under Ulysses S. Grant in the Civil War. In 1864, Parker became Grant's assistant and personal secretary. Parker helped **draft**, or write, the terms of surrender signed by General Robert E. Lee of the Confederate Army at Appomattox Court House, Virginia, ending the war.

Impact of the Civil War

The Civil War lasted four years and was the most destructive war in American history. More than 600,000 Union and Confederate soldiers died. The war had terrible consequences for American Indians living in Indian Territory. One-third of all Cherokees and Seminoles died during the war. Despite the contribution and sacrifice, participation in the war did not protect the American Indian tribal lands or way of life.

 42

Name: _____ Date: _____

Activity: Key Details

Directions: Use the information from the reading selection to complete the graphic organizer.

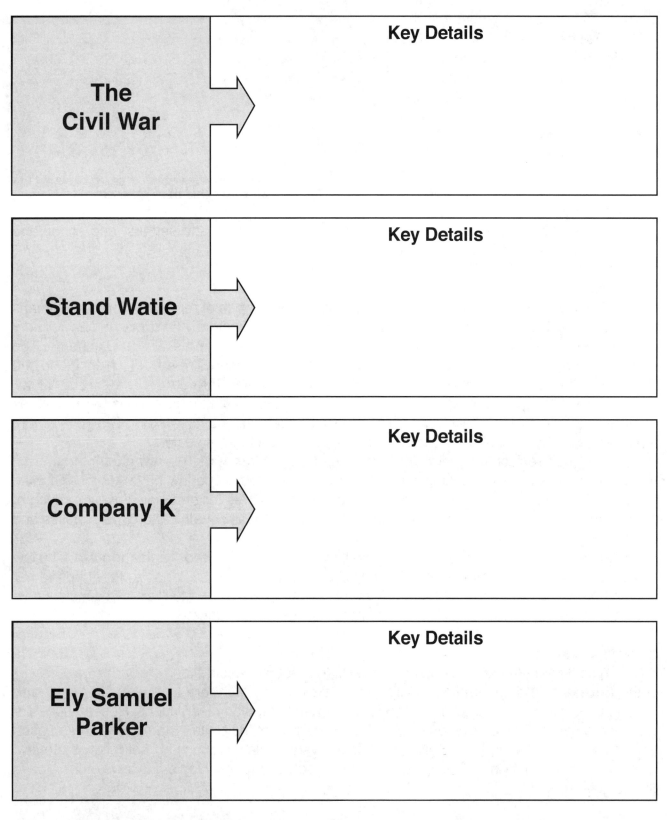

The Civil War

Key Details

Stand Watie

Key Details

Company K

Key Details

Ely Samuel Parker

Key Details

The Indian Reservation System

The **Indian reservation system** was a set of procedures the United States government used to establish and maintain **reservations**, tracts of land set aside for the American Indians. Many reservations were created through various **treaties**, or agreements, between the United States government and American Indian tribes. The purpose of the reservation system was to bring American Indians under the control

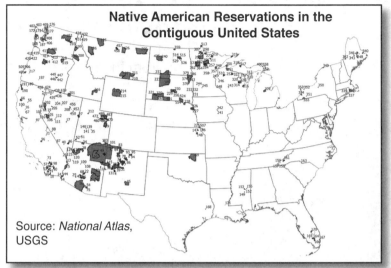

Native American Reservations in the Contiguous United States

Source: *National Atlas*, USGS

There are 35 states that have reservations.

of the United States government, reduce conflict between tribes and settlers, and encourage American Indians to adopt the ways of the white settlers.

Laws and Relocations

The **Indian Removal Act of 1830** established the practice of removing American Indians from their ancestral lands and relocating them to reservations in **Indian Territory**. Indian Territory was located in what are now the present-day states of Kansas, Nebraska, and Oklahoma. The United States government forcibly relocated the **Five Civilized Tribes**, which included the Cherokee, Chickasaw, Choctaw, Creek, and Seminole to Indian Territory.

The **1851 Indian Appropriations Act** set aside government funds to move western tribes onto reservations in Indian Territory. This created the Indian reservation system. The government promised to protect the land American Indians were moved to from settlers.

In 1887, President Grover Cleveland signed the **Dawes Act**. This law attempted to treat American Indians as individuals instead of members of a tribe. The law gave American Indian families 160 acres of reservation land for farming or 320 acres for grazing. However, much of the reservation land was not good farmland, and many families couldn't afford the supplies and equipment needed to plant and harvest crops.

In 1934, President Franklin D. Roosevelt signed the **Indian Reorganization Act**. The law stopped providing reservation lands to families and returned surplus lands to the tribes rather than to homesteaders. It also encouraged tribes to self-govern and write their own constitutions. The government provided financial aid for improving the reservations.

Reservations Today

Indian reservations still exist across the United States. Reservations are under the authority of the **Bureau of Indian Affairs** established in 1824. Today there are 574 federally recognized Indian tribes in the United States. There are 325 American Indian reservations. Reservations are considered nations of their own even though they are part of the United States. Each reservation has its own government, laws, police, and court system. Reservations do not follow state law. However, the people living on reservations do have to obey **federal laws**, the laws of the United States government.

Name: _____   Date: _____

Activity: Recalling Information

Directions: Use the information from the reading selection to complete the page.

Multiple Choice

1. How many states have reservations today?

   A. 535

   B. 35

   C. 0

   D. 50

2. What are tracts of land set aside for American Indians called?

   A. homesteads

   B. farms

   C. reservations

   D. ranches

3. What was the purpose of the Dawes Act of 1887?

4. What was the result of the Indian Removal Act of 1830?

True or False

Write the word TRUE if the statement is correct. If the statement is false, write the word FALSE on the line and underline the word or statement that makes the sentence incorrect. Write the correct answer on the space provided.

_____ 5. The Indian reservation system was a set of procedures the United States government used to establish and maintain reservations.

_____ 6. Reservations are under the authority of the United States Bureau of Land Management.

_____ 7. The Indian Reorganization Act stopped providing American Indian families with 160 acres of reservation land for farming.

Major Conflicts With the United States Army

Many American Indian tribes lived west of the Mississippi River. During the 1800s, railroads, miners, ranchers, and farmers spread westward across the American continent, causing conflicts over land. The United States Army was given the responsibility of protecting the settlers.

Left to right: Geronimo's son, Perico, holding a baby; Geronimo; Natches; unidentified man. This photograph was taken in Geronimo's camp before his surrender to General Crook, March 27, 1886.

American Indians Resist

In 1851, The United States Congress passed the **Indian Appropriations Act**, creating the reservation system. The law recommended moving American Indians to reservations to reduce conflict between them and settlers. **Reservations** were tracts of land set aside for American Indians. It did not solve the problem. Many tribes resisted relocating to new lands. American settlers continued to push westward, and it was not long before they began to move onto reservation land. Conflicts over land became more frequent. Soon, fighting began between the United States Army and various tribes.

The Modoc War of 1872–73: Kintpuash, also known as Captain Jack, and a band of Modoc left the Klamath Reservation in Oregon to return to their original land near the California border. When the Army attempted to take them back to the reservation, fighting broke out. After six months of warfare, the Modoc finally surrendered. Four of their leaders, including Captain Jack, were hanged.

Sioux Wars of 1876–77: The wars were a series of conflicts between the United States and the Sioux people. The Sioux reservation was located in the **Black Hills** of South Dakota. When settlers discovered gold in the Black Hills, miners took over reservation land, causing conflicts. Sitting Bull and Crazy Horse led their people off the reservation. A major battle was fought near the Little Bighorn River in the southern Montana Territory. The Sioux were joined by Cheyenne forces. Lieutenant Colonel George Custer and his troops were killed. The Sioux and Cheyenne won the battle, but within months, government soldiers had forced them to surrender.

Nez Percé War of 1877: The government ordered the Nez Percé to move from eastern Oregon to a smaller reservation in Idaho. The Nez Percé fled the reservation, led by Chief Joseph. They evaded capture for nearly two months before surrendering to United States troops just 40 miles from the Canadian border.

Apache Wars of 1849–1886: After the Mexican American War in 1846, Americans began settling on Apache lands, causing conflicts. As a result, several reservations were created to stop Apache resistance to the takeover of their lands. Leaders such as Cochise and Geronimo gathered hundreds of men and led attacks on settlements that stretched from Arizona to New Mexico. By the 1880s, many Apache bands had agreed to move to reservations. Geronimo and some bands continued the warfare. In 1886, Geronimo and 30 of his men surrendered, ending the Apache Wars.

By the beginning of the 1900s, the United States Army had relocated every American Indian nation to reservations.

Name: Date:

Activity: Summarizing

Directions: Use the information from the reading selection to complete the graphic organizer.

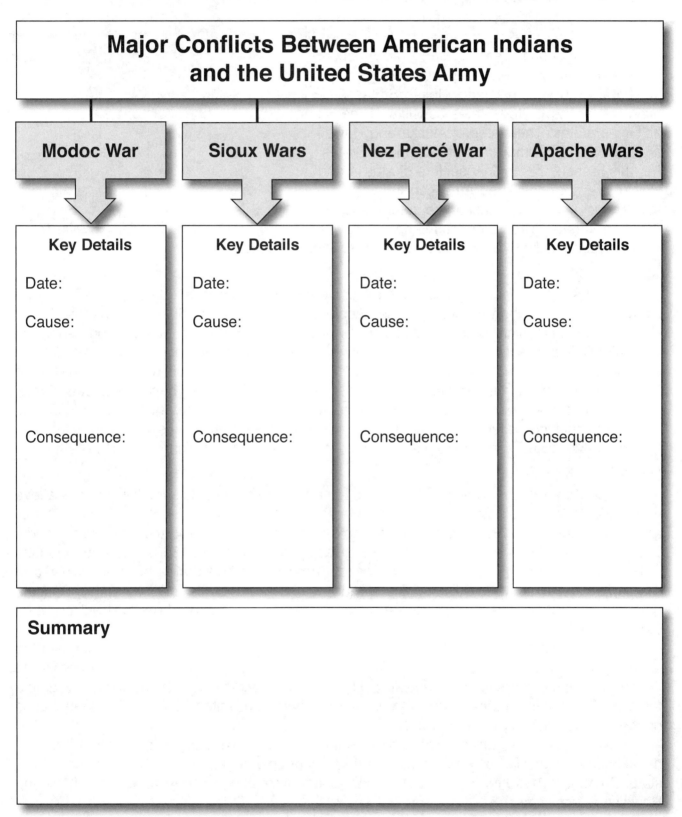

Major Conflicts Between American Indians and the United States Army

Modoc War	Sioux Wars	Nez Percé War	Apache Wars
Key Details Date: Cause: Consequence:	**Key Details** Date: Cause: Consequence:	**Key Details** Date: Cause: Consequence:	**Key Details** Date: Cause: Consequence:

Summary

Alaska and Hawaii

The first people to live in a land are called **indigenous peoples**, or original settlers. **Indigenous Americans** are the original settlers of North and South America. **Native Americans** are the Indigenous Peoples of North America. **American Indian** refers to people living within the **contiguous**, or mainland, United States. The mainland of the United States consists of the 48 adjoining states. The states of Alaska and Hawaii are not part of the mainland of the United States. For this reason, the original settlers of Alaska and Hawaii are not considered American Indians. The Indigenous People of Alaska are referred to as **Alaskan Natives**. The Indigenous People of Hawaii are referred to as **Native Hawaiians and other Pacific Islanders**.

Alaska

Thousands of years ago, during the last Ice Age, people journeyed across a land bridge connecting Asia to North America. These people eventually formed tribes such as the Tlingit, Haida, Aleut, Tsimshian, and the Inuit. Their way of life depended on hunting and fishing. In 1784, the Russians established the first permanent European settlement in Alaska. In 1867, the United States purchased Alaska from Russia for $7.2 million. In 1896, gold was discovered in the Klondike region of Canada. Major gold strikes were also made near what became Juneau, Nome, and Fairbanks, Alaska. Many prospectors and settlers made their way to Alaska. In 1957, oil was discovered, making the territory economically important to the United States. On January 3, 1959, President Dwight D. Eisenhower signed the **Alaska Statehood Act**, making Alaska the 49th state.

Hawaii

The **Polynesians** were the first people to settle the Hawaiian Islands. Historians believe they traveled to Hawaii by canoe from the Marquesas Islands in the southern Pacific Ocean around A.D. 500. In 1778, Captain James Cook from England explored the Hawaiian Islands. Whaling and trading ships started making regular stops. In the mid-1800s, the main industry in Hawaii was farming sugarcane. Many people from the United States became involved in the sugarcane industry. The United States had established friendly relations with the island government, and Americans gradually took control of the sugar industry. They also tried to control the government.

In 1893, **Queen Liliuokalani** was the Hawaiian ruler. She wanted to regain control of the government and restore the ruler's traditional power. Americans living in Hawaii overthrew the government and established the Republic of Hawaii. A few years later, in 1898, Hawaii became a territory of the United States. Over the next several years, the United States built military bases on the islands, including Pearl Harbor.

World War II began in 1939. On December 7, 1941, the Japanese attacked the U.S. naval base at Pearl Harbor. After World War II, many people began to want Hawaii to become a state. On August 21, 1959, President Dwight D. Eisenhower signed **The Admission Act**, making Hawaii the 50th state.

Name: _____   Date: _____

Activity: Compare and Contrast

Directions: Use the information from the reading selection to complete the graphic organizers.

Indigenous Peoples	What is the Difference?	American Indians

Alaska	Date Admitted to the Union
586,412 square miles	Alaska was admitted to the union as our _____ state.

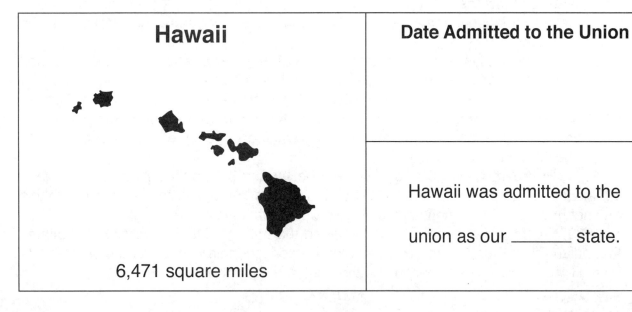

Hawaii	Date Admitted to the Union
6,471 square miles	Hawaii was admitted to the union as our _____ state.

Citizenship

The United States Constitution was signed on September 17, 1787. The document did not explain or define citizenship. In 1868, the 14th Amendment to the Constitution was **ratified**, or approved, defining citizenship. The amendment granted **citizenship** to men over 21 born or naturalized in the United States. **Naturalization** is the process through which an immigrant to the United States can become a U.S. citizen. The amendment also guaranteed citizens certain rights, including the right to vote. However, even though the amendment stated "all persons," it did not mean everyone. Women and American Indians were excluded.

President Calvin Coolidge with four men of the Osage Nation after signing the Indian Citizenship Act

American Indian Rights

In 1778, the United States government began forming treaties with different American Indian tribes. **Treaties** are formal agreements between two nations. The agreements recognized tribes as independent nations within the boundaries of the United States. The treaties recognized the American Indian people as citizens of their tribe. The tribes agreed to give up their rights to hunt and live on parts of their ancestral lands in exchange for trade goods, yearly cash payments, and the promise that no further demands would be made on them.

The treaties led to a policy of **Indian removal**. After 1830, American Indians found themselves being confined to reservations. The **reservation system** was a set of procedures the United States government used to establish and maintain **reservations**, tracts of land set aside for the American Indians to live on. Under the reservation system, American Indians kept their citizenship in their independent tribes, but they were forced to live on land set aside by the United States government.

In 1871, President Ulysses S. Grant signed the **Indian Appropriation Act**. The law ended recognizing tribes as nations and declared previous treaties with the tribes no longer valid.

During World War I (1914–1918), over 9,000 Native Americans served in the United States military. In 1919, President Woodrow Wilson signed the **American Indian Citizenship Act**. The law authorized those American Indian veterans who wanted to become American citizens to apply for and be granted citizenship.

In 1924, President Calvin Coolidge signed the **Indian Citizenship Act**. The law gave American Indians full citizenship in the United States, including the right to vote. Even with this law, it was not until 1948 that American Indians were allowed to vote in every state.

In 1968, President Lyndon B. Johnson signed the **Indian Civil Rights Act**, sometimes called the Indian Bill of Rights. This law guaranteed American Indians many of the same rights in the Bill of Rights, such as free speech and the right to a speedy and fair trial.

Activity: Timeline

Directions: Use the information from the reading selection to complete the timeline. Explain each event on the timeline.

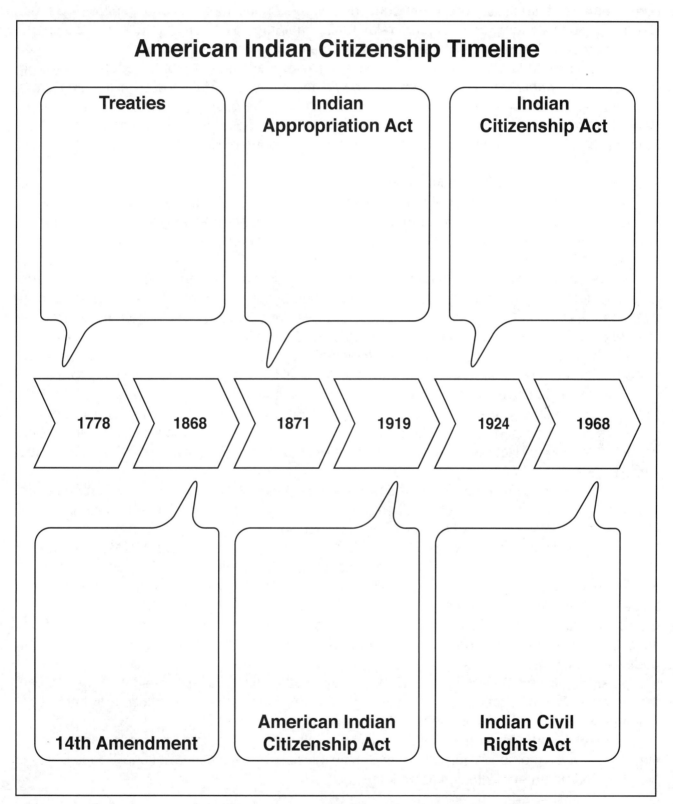

American Indian Citizenship Timeline

Treaties	Indian Appropriation Act	Indian Citizenship Act

1778 → 1868 → 1871 → 1919 → 1924 → 1968

14th Amendment	American Indian Citizenship Act	Indian Civil Rights Act

American Indians Who Made a Difference

Native Americans have made many valuable contributions to the American way of life. Many of the foods we eat today were first grown by Native Americans, such as potatoes, beans, corn, peanuts, pumpkins, tomatoes, squash, peppers, nuts, melons, and sunflower seeds. Canoeing, snowshoeing, tobogganing, relay racing, and tug-of-war are just a few of the sports and games early Native Americans played that Americans still enjoy today.

American Indian words have become an everyday part of our language, including *barbecue, chipmunk, skunk, hammock, hurricane,* and *moccasin.* Many towns, cities, and rivers have names of American Indian origin including Seattle, Milwaukee, Miami, and Mississippi. Benjamin Franklin said the idea for the structuring of the United States government was borrowed from the system of government used by the Iroquoian League of Nations.

American Indians Excelled in Many Fields

Sequoya was a member of the Cherokee Nation. In 1821, Sequoya invented an alphabet so his people could read and write in their language. The Cherokee began to teach it in their schools. They also published books and newspapers in their own language. The sequoia tree was named in his honor.

Ely Samuel Parker was a member of the Seneca Nation. During the Civil War, he served as General Ulysses S. Grant's secretary and adviser. When the Confederates surrendered at Appomattox Court House, Virginia, on April 9,1865, Parker helped to draft the terms of surrender for General Robert E. Lee to sign. Parker was given the rank of brigadier general for his work. He was the first American Indian to earn the rank of brigadier general in the United States Army. In 1869, he became the first American Indian to work as the Commissioner for Indian Affairs.

Charles D. Curtis was a member of the Kaw Nation. In 1893, he was the first American Indian to be elected to the United States House of Representatives. In 1907, he was the first American Indian elected to the United States Senate. In March 1929, he was sworn in as vice president to Herbert Hoover. Charles Curtis was the first Native American Vice President of the United States.

Jim Thorpe was a member of the Sac and Fox Nation. In 1911, he was the first American Indian to play in the National Football League. In 1912, Thorpe was the first American Indian to win gold medals for the United States in the Olympic Games.

The **code talkers** were 29 Navajo men who joined the United States Marines during World War II. In 1942, they created a code using the Navajo language. The code was used to keep military secrets during the war. By the end of the war, there were approximately 400 Native Code Talkers in the military from the Navajo, Cherokee, Choctaw, Lakota, Meskwaki, and Comanche code talkers. Each translated coded messages in their native tongues from the front lines. The code talkers played a key role in the United States' victory over Japan in 1945. Their code was never broken.

Annie Dodge Wauneka was of the Navajo Nation. In 1963, she was the first American Indian to receive the Presidential Medal of Freedom. Wauneaka was recognized for her efforts to improve health care among the Navajo people.

In 2002, **John Herrington** of the Chickasaw Nation was the first America Indian in space. Herrington was a member of the sixteenth Shuttle mission to visit the International Space Station. He was the first American Indian to walk in space.

Activity: Locating Information

Directions: Use the information from the reading selection to complete the chart.

Notable American Indians			
Name	**Nation/Tribe**	**Date**	**Contribution**
Sequoya			
Ely Samuel Parker			
Charles D. Curtis			
Jim Thorpe			
Code Talkers			
Annie Dodge Wauneka			
John Herrington			

Vice President Charles Curtis

Charles Curtis was the first American Indian vice president. Curtis served as the 31st vice president of the United States from 1929 to 1933 with President Herbert Hoover.

Charles Curtis, who was of Native American descent, was the 31st vice president of the United States.

Early Life

Charles Curtis was born on January 25, 1860, in North Topeka, Kansas Territory. His mother, Ellen Papin, was of American Indian descent: Kaw, Osage, and Potawatomi. His father, Orren Curtis, was of European ancestry. Charles' mother died in 1863 when he was three years old. Growing up, he lived on the Kaw reservation with his grandparents. Curtis married Annie Elizabeth Baird on November 27, 1884. They had three children. Annie died in 1924. Curtis was unmarried during his term as vice president of the United States.

Curtis Enters Politics

Curtis served in the United States House of Representatives from 1893 to 1907, the first American Indian to be elected to the House. He drafted what became known as the **Curtis Act of 1898**, abolishing tribal courts and subjecting all persons in the Indian territory to federal law.

Curtis was also the first American Indian to be elected to the Senate. He served two terms as the United States senator from Kansas from 1907 to 1913 and then from 1915 to 1929. Curtis was instrumental in the 1919 passing of the **19th Amendment** to the U.S. Constitution by Congress. The amendment granted women the right to vote. He served as the majority leader of the Senate from 1924 to 1929.

Vice President Curtis

Curtis ran as the running mate for Republican presidential candidate Herbert Hoover in 1928. They won a landslide victory over Democrats Al Smith and Joseph T. Robinson. Curtis served as the 31st vice president of the United States from 1929 to 1933.

Curtis' election as vice president made history because he was the only native Kansan and the only American Indian to hold the post. Curtis decorated his office with Native American artifacts and often posed for pictures by wearing an American Indian headdress.

The Stock Market Crash in 1929 led to what is known as **The Great Depression**. This was a time when many banks failed, many people lost their homes, and many farmers lost their land. In 1932, President Hoover and Vice President Curtis ran together seeking re-election. The public, wanting new leadership, elected Democrats Franklin D. Roosevelt and John Nance Garner. Charles Curtis' term as vice president ended on March 4, 1933.

After Politics

After leaving office in 1933, Charles Curtis returned to the practice of law in Washington, D.C. On February 8, 1936, he suffered a fatal heart attack. He was buried in Topeka, Kansas.

Name: Date:

Activity: Textual Evidence

Directions: Use information from the reading selection to answer the questions below. Support your answers with details and examples from the reading selection.

1. Who was Charles Curtis?

2. What was the purpose of the Curtis Act of 1898?

3. Which events led to the loss of reelection for President Herbert Hoover and Vice President Charles Curtis in 1932?

National American Indian Heritage Month

Arthur C. Parker

The history of Native Americans is vital to the history of our nation from exploration and settlement to the present day. **National American Indian Heritage Month** is a time to learn about and remember the important accomplishments and contributions that the first people to live here made to the United States. Many states and cities hold festivals, dances, and theater performances to celebrate Native American Heritage Month in November.

First Americans Day

Dr. Arthur C. Parker was a member of the Seneca Nation. Parker was the director of the Museum of Arts and Science in Rochester, New York, from 1924 to 1945. He was an authority on American Indian culture. He was also the great-nephew of Ely Samuel Parker, the first American Indian to be Commissioner of Indian Affairs. In 1912, he convinced the Boy Scouts of America to set aside a day for the "First Americans." The Boy Scouts celebrated **First Americans Day** for three years.

A Day to Honor American Indians

In 1914, the Reverend Red Fox James, a member of the Blackfeet and Crow Nations rode on horseback from Montana to Washington, D.C. He hoped to persuade President Woodrow Wilson to create a national holiday to recognize the culture, traditions, and contributions of the American Indians to the United States. The cross-country ride brought national attention to the issue, but no action from the president.

In 1915, the Congress of the American Indian Association asked that a day be established to recognize American Indian heritage. On September 18, 1915, the group's president, Reverend Sherman Coolidge, issued a **proclamation**, or statement, declaring the second Saturday of each May as **American Indian Day** and appealing for U.S. citizenship for American Indians. In May 1916, the first American Indian Day was celebrated in New York.

American Indian Week

After 1916, days of recognition for Native Americans began popping up across the United States, but there still was not a national day dedicated to Native American heritage. In 1976, during celebration of the nation's 200th birthday, President Gerald Ford proclaimed October 10–16, **Native American Awareness Week**. In 1986, Ronald Reagan changed Native American Awareness Week to November 23–30.

National American Indian Heritage Month

In 1990, President George H. W. Bush signed a law extending American Indian Week to a month. He changed the name of the celebration to **National American Indian Heritage Month**, also known as Native American Heritage Month. It is now observed in November.

Native American Heritage Day

In 2009, President Barack Obama signed "The Native American Heritage Day Resolution." The law authorized the Friday after Thanksgiving as **Native American Heritage Day**.

Indigenous Peoples' Day

Indigenous Peoples' Day is also celebrated in many states and cities on the second Monday in October. President Joe Biden was the first president to issue a presidential proclamation recognizing the holiday in 2021.

Name: _____   Date: _____

Activity: Summarizing

Directions: Use the information from the reading selection to summarize each event.

1.

First Americans Day

2.

Native American Awareness Week

3.

National American Indian Heritage Month

Answer Keys

Note: Some answers may vary. Suggested answers are given, but students may have other valid answers. Teacher check for appropriate responses.

Unit One: Indigenous People of North America
Prehistoric Migration to the Americas: Cause and Effect (p. 3)
Map
1. Bering Land Bridge
2. From the northwest to the south and east

<u>Causes</u>: During the last ice age, the levels of the oceans lowered because much of the earth's water was trapped in the giant polar ice caps. The lower water level exposed a piece of land between Asia and North America. This land bridge was a thousand miles wide. Scientists believe the land bridge was free of ice and covered in grass. During this time, herds of hairy elephants called mammoths and giant bison from Asia came to graze. Early people depended on animals for their food, clothing, and shelter. They followed the grass-eating animals across the land bridge.

<u>Effects</u>: During the last ice age, animals and people migrated from Asia to North America. As they traveled, groups might have settled for a time in a place that offered good hunting or fishing. Eventually, some of the groups or their descendants continued the journey, following the migrating herds of animals they hunted into the eastern parts of North America and as far south as the tip of South America.

Early Cultures and Civilizations: Locating Information (p. 5)
1. Mound Builders
2. Ancestral Pueblo
3. Hohokam
4. Aztec Empire
5. Mayan Empire
6. Inca Empire
Fill in the Blanks
1. culture
2. civilization

Native American Cultural Regions: Locating Information (p. 7)
Multiple Choice
1. C   2. D
Fill in the Blanks
1. indigenous
2. cultural
3. tribes
4. pyramids
True or False
1. True
2. False; The <u>California</u> tribes were known as the "seed gatherers of the desert."
3. False; The Woodland tribes lived in <u>wood houses</u>. or The <u>Pueblo</u> tribes lived in houses made of adobe.

Unit Two: The New World
The Age of Exploration: Cause and Effect (p. 9)
1. Land trade routes to the Far East were shut down.

2. In 1488, Bartolomeu Dias of Portugal led the first European expedition around the southern tip of Africa. This opened the way for sea trade between Europe and the Far East.
3. Spain received most of the Americas while Portugal received the land now known as Brazil in South America. The treaty also gave Spain and Portugal the right to claim any land of any people they conquered in the Americas.
4. In 1521, Hernan Cortés conquered the Aztec in present-day Mexico and seized control of the region. In 1532, Francisco Pizarro conquered the Inca in present-day Peru and claimed the land for Spain.

First Contact: Key Details (p. 11)
<u>Jacques Cartier</u> was a French explorer looking for the Northwest Passage. In 1534, he made contact with members of the Iroquois Nation. He kidnapped Chief Donnacona's two sons and took them back to France. He returned them on his second trip in 1535. Cartier then captured Donnacona and took him to France, where Donnacona died. On his third trip in 1541, he brought French settlers to establish a colony. When the Iroquois people realized the French intended to settle, they became unfriendly.

<u>Sir Francis Drake</u> was an English explorer. In 1580, he became the first Englishman to navigate the Straits of Magellan. Drake then sailed north along the coast of the Americas and landed near present-day San Francisco Bay, claiming the land for England. There he met and made friends with the Coastal Miwok. He continued the voyage and became the first Englishman to circumnavigate the globe.

<u>Sir Walter Raleigh</u> was an English explorer. In 1585, he sent ships to explore the Atlantic Coast of North America and establish a settlement. The ship landed on Roanoke Island, part of the territory of the Carolina Algonquian-speaking people, known as the Roanoke. The Roanoke Island colony suffered from a food shortage and attacks by the Roanoke so the colonists returned to England in 1586. A second group arrived in 1587, but these colonists had all disappeared by the time a supply ship arrived from England in 1590.

<u>Samuel de Champlain</u> was a French explorer who made many trips to North America to find the Northwest Passage. In 1608, he established the first permanent French colony in North America, the city of Quebec on the St. Lawrence River. Champlain became an ally of the Algonquins and Hurons against the Iroquois to protect the French fur-trading interests.

<u>Henry Hudson</u> was an English explorer. Starting in 1607, he conducted four different expeditions searching for the Northwest Passage. On his third voyage, he worked for the Dutch and explored the river he called the

Hudson River. Hudson traded with the Mohicans, and he was able to bring back corn, tobacco, and valuable furs to the Netherlands. His successful fur trading with the Mohicans led to more Europeans wanting to come and trade as well.

René Robert Cavalier de La Salle was a French explorer searching for a water route to Asia. In 1682, he was the first European to navigate the Mississippi River to the Gulf of Mexico. His friendships with numerous Native American tribes assisted and supported French colonial settlers and the military up to the French and Indian War of 1754.

Spanish Missions: Summarizing (p. 13)

The Spanish Colonial Empire: Spain had the largest of the colonial empires in the New World. It comprised several islands in the West Indies, all of Mexico, most of Central America and South America, and what are now Florida, California, and the United States Southwest.

Spanish Missions: Spanish missions were religious communities in North America. Spain used missions to convert and control Native Americans and ensure rival countries didn't try to occupy land claimed by Spain.

Native American Resistance: Frequent rebellions rocked the missions of what would become Texas, New Mexico, southern Arizona, and California. From 1599–1620, tribes of the Sierra Madres rebelled. The Pueblo Rebellion erupted in 1680. It ended Spanish rule in New Mexico for 12 years. In 1775, the Tipai-Ipai attacked the mission at San Diego. Revolts ended with many deaths of missionaries, settlers, and Native Americans.

Summary: Spain had the largest of the colonial empires in the New World. Spanish missions were religious communities in North America. Spain used missions to convert and control Native Americans and ensure rival countries didn't try to occupy land claimed by Spain. Native American revolts ended with many deaths on both sides. In 1821, Mexico won independence from Spain. In 1833, the Mexican government ended missions.

The Powhatan Confederacy: Textual Evidence (p. 15)

1. The Algonquian people shared the same language and culture. They lived by hunting, trapping, and fishing and gathering roots, nuts, wild rice, fruit, and berries. Many groups also grew corn, beans, and squash. Some tribes also grew tobacco.
2. The Powhatan Confederacy was a union of 30 of the Algonquian-speaking tribes that occupied the coast of Virginia, Chesapeake Bay, and southern Maryland. This confederacy was formed by the powerful chief of the Powhatan tribe, Wahunsenacah, also known as Powhatan.
3. After the Jamestown settlers demanded food in 1609, war broke out and the Powhatan people laid siege to James Fort. Later, new English settlements

and profitable tobacco trade pushed the Powhatan people off their land. As a result, the Powhatan people launched a series of attacks on the English to drive them from the area.
4. Opechancanough was captured and killed. In 1646, a treaty dissolved the Powhatan Confederacy and gave most of their land to the English colonists.

The Wampanoag Confederacy: Cause and Effect (p. 17)

1. The Wampanoag helped the English colony of Plymouth survive in the New World.
2. The Wampanoag suffered from an epidemic between 1616 and 1619 of smallpox introduced by contact with Europeans. The time is known as the "Great Dying." Entire villages disappeared, and only a fraction of the Wampanoag population survived.
3. After an exchange of greetings and gifts, Chief Massasoit and leaders of the Plymouth settlement signed the Pilgrim-Wampanoag Peace Treaty. The treaty lasted for more than 50 years.
4. Chief Metacom led an uprising to drive out the English colonists known as King Philip's War. During the 14-month conflict, thousands of Native Americans were killed, wounded, or captured. The Wampanoag tribe was destroyed by the English. Metacom fled to Mount Hope in present-day Bristol, Rhode Island, where he was killed by the English.

Unit Three: Trouble on the Frontier
The Iroquois Confederacy: Textual Evidence (p. 19)

1. The original Iroquois tribes were the Cayuga, Mohawk, Oneida, Onondaga, and Seneca. The Tuscarora tribe joined later.
2. Beaver pelts were in great demand in Europe. Native American tribes would hunt game animals and trade the pelts with the Europeans. The French, British, and Dutch competed against each other to get these pelts.
3. The Iroquois Confederacy took control of the fur trade. They defeated the Huron, attacked French settlements and Algonquian-speaking tribes. Many tribes, including the Shawnee, were forced from their homelands. The French and their allies attacked Iroquois villages and English settlements.

French and Indian War: Citing Evidence (p. 21)

Causes: French, English, and Native Americans claimed the Ohio River Valley. In 1754, George Washington and 150 Virginia militia were sent to drive out the French. Skirmishes between British colonists and the French and their American Indian allies led to the French and Indian War.

Effects: France and Spain lost the war. The Treaty of Paris was signed in 1763. England received Florida from Spain and all French territory east of the Mississippi except New Orleans. English colonists moved

West. The British regarded the American Indians as conquered peoples rather than allies. Tensions erupted into a frontier war, known as Pontiac's War

Pontiac's War: Locating Information (p. 23)

<u>Settlement to the West</u>: British colonists expand their settlements west from the Appalachian Mountains to the Mississippi River.

<u>Pontiac's War</u>: Chief Pontiac and a confederation of Native Americans dissatisfied with British rule in the Great Lakes raided settlements in the area.

<u>Proclamation of 1763</u>: King George III forbade any English settlements west of the Appalachian Mountains.

<u>Treaty of Oswego</u>: The treaty brought an official end to Pontiac's War in 1766. Pontiac received a pardon for his role in the affair.

The American Revolution: Locating Information (p. 25)

1. The American Revolutionary War was fought from 1775 until 1783 between the British and American colonists.
2. King George III and the British parliament decided to raise money to pay for the cost of the French and Indian War by taxing the American colonists. The taxes made many of the colonists angry because they had no representation in Parliament to vote against the taxes or speak for the interests of the colonies.
3. Some American Indian nations stayed neutral. Most of the nations sided with the British. A few allied with the colonists. Many who took part in the war conducted raids on supply lines, attacked settlements, and fought alongside soldiers in numerous battles throughout the war.
4. Britain recognized the independence of the United States. The new nation received all the territory between the Atlantic Ocean and the Mississippi River and between the Great Lakes and Florida. The American Indians were considered a conquered people throughout the entire country and were eventually forced to give up most of their land.

The Northwestern Confederacy: Locating Information (p. 27)

1. The United States and the Northwestern Confederacy both wanted to control the Northwest Territory.
2. The Northwestern Confederacy was a union of American Indian tribes in the Great Lakes region of the United States: Miami, Shawnee, Lenape (Delaware), Mingo, Wyandot, Cherokee, Ottawa, Ojibwa, and Potawatomi.
3. Michikinikwa was a leader of the Miami people of the Great Lakes region during the 1700s. He was a leader of the Northwestern Confederacy, known as Little Turtle to the English.

4. On August 20, 1794, Blue Jacket and his followers were defeated at the Battle of Fallen Timbers, ending the war.
5. The Treaty of Greenville in 1795 ended the Northwest Indian War.

Tecumseh: Key Details (p. 29)

1. The Battle of Fallen Timbers was a conflict between the Shawnee tribe, settlers, and the United States military in 1794. It resulted in a victory for the United States. The battle ended the Northwest Indian War, also known as Little Turtle's War.
2. In 1795, the Treaty of Greenville was signed. Tecumseh disputed the treaty over the surrender of tribal lands and refused to sign. After, Tecumseh tried to unite Ohio Valley nations against settlers.
3. The Ohio Valley Confederacy united the Shawnee, Potawatomi, Kickapoo, Winnebago, Menominee, Ottawa, and Wyandot nations.
4. The War of 1812 was fought by the United States and its American Indian allies against the United Kingdom and its American Indian allies. It was a conflict over trade practices. Tecumseh was killed. In 1814, Great Britain and the United States signed the Treaty of Ghent, ending the war.

Unit Three: Westward Migration
American Indian Cultures of the West: Categorizing Information (p. 31)

<u>Plains</u>: west-central region between the Mississippi River and the Rocky Mountains; Comanche, Sioux, and Blackfoot; tipis; buffalo

<u>Southwest</u>: southwestern region of the United States and northern Mexico; Pueblo, Apache, and Navajo; Pueblo—adobe pueblos, Navajo—hogans, Apache—wickiups; farming, hunting, and gathering

<u>Plateau</u>: between the Rocky Mountains and the Cascade Mountain Range; Nez Percé, Flathead, and Yakama; tipis; roots, berries, and wild game

<u>Northwest</u>: along the coast of Pacific Ocean; Chinook, Haida, and Tlingit; rectangular homes made of cedar; hunting, fishing, seeds, berries, and nuts

<u>Great Basin</u>: west-central region of the United States and Canada; Shoshone, Ute, and Paiute; brush windbreaks in the summer and wickiups in the winter; roots, seeds, nuts, salmon, bison, deer, elk, and mountain sheep

<u>California</u>: California and northern part of the Mexican state of Baja California; Chumash, Promo, and Yuma; most typical home was a wickiup; berries, nuts, seeds, and roots and wild game such as rabbits and deer

Manifest Destiny: Locating Information (p. 33)

<u>Definition</u>: a belief that the growth of the United States was both a right and an obligation

<u>Problems</u>: armed conflict between American Indians and settlers and the United States Army

1. In 1803, the United States purchased the Louisiana

Territory from France for $15 million. The purchase doubled the size of the United States.

2. In 1845, the republic of Texas was annexed, or taken over, by the United States, and it became the 28th state.

3. In 1846, a treaty established the 49th parallel as the border of the United States and British-owned Canada. In 1848, Congress formally established the land as the Oregon Territory.

4. After the Mexican American War, Mexico gave the United States land referred to as the Mexican Cession. The territory was organized as California and the Utah Territory and New Mexico Territory.

5. The United States purchased land from Mexico along the southern edge of the present-day states of Arizona and New Mexico for $10 million. The purchase established the Mexico-United States border.

Sacagawea and the Corps of Discovery: Locating Information (p. 35)

Who: a Shoshone woman who accompanied the Corps of Discovery

What: an expedition to explore the Louisiana Territory and find a water route from the Missouri River leading west to the Pacific Ocean

When and Where: 1804 to 1806; St. Louis to the Pacific Ocean

How: She was an interpreter with other American Indians. She helped bargain for horses. She saved papers, intruments, and medicines from being lost in the river.

The Five Civilized Tribes: Timeline (p. 37)

1825: In 1825, Congress reserved the land for the resettlement of Native Americans to the west of the Mississippi River as Indian Territory.

1830: President Jackson signed the Indian Removal Act.

1831: The forced removal of the Choctaw to land in the Indian Territory began.

1835: Seminole War

1836: The Creeks were forced from their homes and relocated in Indian Territory.

1838: 17,000 Cherokee began the forced relocation journey to present-day Oklahoma on what came to be called the Trail of Tears.

American Indians Struggle: Cause and Effect (p. 39)

1. 1803: The size of the United States doubled.
2. 1848: People from all over the world swarmed to California.
3. 1862: It opened the West to homesteaders.
4. 1869: It made it possible to travel from the east coast to the west coast of the nation in one week.
5. 1890: Congress broke a 60-year-old pledge to preserve land in Indian Territory exclusively for

Native Americans forced from their lands in the east.

6. 1890s: 1.9 million acres of land in Unassigned Indian Territory was claimed by white settlers.

The American Bison: Locating Information (p. 41)

1. B   2. D   3. Buffalo Bill Cody
4. Great Plains and prairies from the Rocky Mountains east to the Mississippi River, and from the Great Lakes to Texas
5. Demand by Europeans for buffalo robes; Homestead Act of 1862; destroy bison to defeat American Indians; construction of the Transcontinental Railroads; bison-killing contests (any four)

The Civil War: Key Details (p. 43)

The Civil War: from 1861 to 1865; conflict over states' rights and slavery

Stand Watie: Cherokee Colonel in the Confederate Army; led regiment in Battle of Pea Ridge; led his troops in 18 battles and major skirmishes; last Confederate general to surrender

Company K: Native American unit of sharpshooters in the Union Army

Ely Samuel Parker: Seneca leader; fought at Vicksburg under Ulysses S. Grant; secretary to Grant; helped draft the terms of surrender signed by Robert E. Lee at Appomattox Court House to end the war

The Indian Reservation System: Recalling Information (p. 45)

1. B   2. C
3. turn American Indians into farmers and landowners
4. removing American Indians from their ancestral lands and relocating them on reservations
5. True
6. False: Reservations are under the authority of the Bureau of Indian Affairs.
7. True

Major Conflicts With the United States Army: Summarizing (p. 47)

Modoc War: 1872–1873; Captain Jack and a band of Modoc left the Klamath Reservation in Oregon to return to their home near the California border.; After 6 months of warfare, the Modoc finally surrendered. Four Modoc leaders, including Captain Jack, were hanged.

Sioux Wars: 1876–1877; Settlers discovered gold in the Black Hills, miners swarmed onto the reservations, and Sitting Bull and Crazy Horse led their people off the reservation.; The Sioux were joined by Cheyenne forces. Lieutenant Colonel George Custer and his troops were killed. The Sioux and Cheyenne won the battle, but within months, government soldiers had forced them to surrender.

Nez Percé War: 1877; Nez Percé were going to be forced from Oregon to a smaller reservation in Idaho. The Nez Percé fled the reservation and evaded capture for nearly two months before surrendering to United

States troops just 40 miles from the Canadian border.

Apache Wars:1849–1889: Americans began settling on Apache lands. Reservations were created to stop resistance to the occupation of Apache lands; In the 1880s many Apache bands agreed to a settlement with the government and moved to reservations. Geronimo and some bands continued the warfare. In 1886, Geronimo and 30 of his men surrendered, ending the Apache Wars.

Summary: In 1851, The United States Congress passed the Indian Appropriations Act, creating the reservation system. The law recommended moving American Indians to reservations to reduce conflict between them and settlers. Many tribes such as the Modoc, Sioux, Nez Percé, and Apache resisted relocation and confinement on reservations. By the beginning of the 1900s, the United States Army had relocated every American Indian nation to reservations.

Alaska and Hawaii: Compare and Contrast (p. 49)

Indigenous Peoples: first people to settle in a land

American Indians: indigenous peoples of the contiguous United States

Alaska: January 3, 1959; 49th

Hawaii: August 21, 1959; 50th

Unit Four: American Indian Achievements
Citizenship: Timeline (p. 51)

1778: The United States government began forming treaties with different American Indian tribes. The agreements recognized tribes as independent nations within the boundaries of the United States.

1868: The amendment defined citizenship but did not include American Indians.

1871: The law ended recognizing tribes as nations and declared previous treaties with the tribes no longer valid.

1919: The law authorized those American Indian veterans who wanted to become American citizens to apply for and be granted citizenship.

1924: The law gave American Indians full citizenship in the United States, including the right to vote.

1968: This law guaranteed American Indians many of the same rights that are in the Bill of Rights such as free speech and the right to a speedy and fair trial.

American Indians Who Made a Difference: Locating Information (p. 53)

Sequoya: Cherokee; 1821; invented a system of writing Cherokee language

Ely Samuel Parker: Seneca; 1865; helped to draft the terms of surrender for Gen. Robert E. Lee to sign; 1869; the first American Indian to work as the Commissioner for Indian Affairs

Charles D. Curtis: Kaw; 1893; first American Indian elected to House of Representatives; 1907; first American Indian elected to the Senate; 1929; first

American Indian vice president of the United States.

Jim Thorpe: Sac and Fox; 1912; the first Native American to win gold medals for the United States in the Olympic Games

Code Talkers: Navajo, Cherokee, Choctaw, Lakota, Meskwaki, and Comanche; 1942–1945; created a code using their native languages to send messages during the war

Annie Dodge Wauneka: Navajo; 1963; first American Indian to receive the Presidential Medal of Freedom; recognized for her efforts to improve health care among her people

John Herrington: Chickasaw; 2002; first Native American in space, first Native American to walk in space

Vice President Charles Curtis: Textual Evidence (p. 55)

1. Charles Curtis was the first American Indian Vice President. Curtis served as the 31st vice president of the United States from 1929 to 1933 with President Herbert Hoover. He was also the first American Indian elected to the House and the Senate.

2. While serving in the United States House of Representatives from 1893 to 1907, Curtis drafted what became known as the Curtis Act of 1898, abolishing tribal courts and subjecting all persons in the Indian Territory to federal law.

3. The Stock Market Crash in 1929 led to what is known as The Great Depression. This was a time when many banks failed, many people lost their homes, and many farmers lost their land. In 1932, President Hoover and Vice President Curtis ran together seeking re-election. The public, wanting new leadership, elected Franklin Roosevelt and John Nance Garner.

National American Indian Heritage Month: Summarizing (p. 57)

1. Dr. Arthur C. Parker was a member of the Seneca Nation. Parker was the director of the Museum of Arts and Science in Rochester, New York. In 1912, he persuaded the Boy Scouts of America to set aside a day for the "First Americans." The Boy Scouts celebrated "First Americans Day" for three years.

2. In 1976, during the celebration of the nation's 200th birthday, President Gerald Ford proclaimed October 10–16, Native American Awareness Week. In 1986, Ronald Reagan changed Native American Awareness Week from October 10–16 to November 23–30.

3. In 1990, President George H. W. Bush signed a law extending the American Indian Week to a month. He changed the name of the celebration to National American Indian Heritage Month, also known as Native American Heritage Month. It is now observed in November.